PADDLE YOUR OWN
KAYAK

AN ILLUSTRATED GUIDE TO THE ART OF KAYAKING

PADDLE YOUR OWN KAYAK

AN ILLUSTRATED GUIDE TO THE ART OF KAYAKING

GARY & JOANIE MCGUFFIN

The BOSTON
MILLS PRESS

A BOSTON MILLS PRESS BOOK

First printing 2008

Library and Archives Canada Cataloguing in Publication

McGuffin, Gary
Paddle your own kayak : an illustrated guide to the art of kayaking / Gary & Joanie McGuffin.

ISBN-10: 1-55046-464-7   ISBN-13: 978-1-55046-464-1
1. Kayaking--Guidebooks. I. McGuffin, Joanie II. Title.
GV783.M384 2008   797.1'224   C2007-907301-8

Publisher Cataloging-in-Publication Data (U.S.)

McGuffin, Gary
Paddle your own kayak : an illustrated guide to the art of kayaking / Gary & Joanie McGuffin.
[208] p. : col. illus., col. photos. ; cm.
Includes bibliographical references and index.

Summary: A guide to kayaking, including history, equipment, carrying and launching, step-by-step instruction on strokes and maneuvers, safety, rescues, kayak camping, tripping, weather, waves and navigation.

ISBN-10: 1-55046-464-7   ISBN-13: 978-1-55046-464-1
1. Kayaking. I. McGuffin, Joanie II. Title.
797.1' 224 dc22   GV783.M348 2008

Published by Boston Mills Press, 2008
132 Main Street, Erin, Ontario, Canada N0B 1T0
Tel: 519-833-2407 • Fax: 519-833-2195
e-mail: books@bostonmillspress.com
www.bostonmillspress.com

In Canada
Distributed by Firefly Books Ltd.
66 Leek Crescent, Richmond Hill
Ontario, Canada L4B 1H1

In the United States
Distributed by Firefly Books (U.S.) Inc.
P.O. Box 1338, Ellicott Station
Buffalo, New York, USA 14205

The publisher gratefully acknowledges the financial support for our publishing program by the Government of Canada through the Book Publishing Industry Development Program (BPIDP).

Design by Chris McCorkindale and Sue Breen, McCorkindale Advertising & Design
Illustrations by Joanie McGuffin and coloring by Iles Guran.
Vector illustrations by Brent Mulligan.
Editor, Kathleen Fraser.
Printed in China

All photographs by Gary and Joanie McGuffin unless otherwise noted.

Front cover, clockwise: Family kayaking near Killarney; whitewater on the Serpent River; exploring Greenland's icebergs; an assisted rescue in action; kayak camping; practicing the high-brace U-turn.
Back cover: Georgian Bay.
Half-title page: Discovering Nuuk Fjord with a Greenlandic friend.
Title page: Near Philip Edward Island.
Opposite: Batchawana Bay.
Page 6: Evening view of the La Cloche Mountains.

For Sila

CONTENTS

CHAPTER 1

THE WAY OF THE KAYAK

NO MATTER WHERE WE LIVE, the physical environment we grow up in inscribes its mark upon each of us very early in life. If that place is close to nature, and we have the opportunity and encouragement to be influenced in a pleasurable way by nature, its magic stays within us for the rest of our lives. For Gary and me, our landscape has been the clear lakes and rivers of Canada. What endures from our earliest memories is much more than what we have seen of these places. We recall the engagement of all our senses: the cool thrill of refreshing swims on hot summer nights, the sharp scents of pine and cedar forest, the unmistakable sound of loon calls echoing across the calm, the crack and boom of thunderstorms and the changeable forces of wind and water along the shore, from rhythmic ripples lapping at our toes to giant green waves pounding against the granite coast of the largest freshwater lake in the world.

And then there were boats. We can both remember paddle-powered travel in canoes from a very young age. When we were teenagers, we were each introduced to kayaking — whitewater kayaks for river travel and touring kayaks for exploring our "backyard" lake systems in Temagami and Muskoka. In each of our experiences, we quickly discovered that being a kayaker offered a whole different feel to travel in places already familiar from canoe explorations.

A memorable evening: the warmth of the fire, mugs of hot tea, and our daughter in the tent singing to herself.

No place takes you closer to the heart of the kayak's heritage than Greenland, where snow brightens the mountains on a summer day.

The action in using a double-bladed kayak paddle seemed to us to have a balanced, meditative quality about it, more so than the action of a single-blade canoe paddle. The lower center of gravity in a kayak made it very stable and brought us closer to the water, making us feel part of it. Our kayaks skimmed over the surface effortlessly as we cruised along familiar shorelines of ponds, lakeshores and coastlines and reached new vistas. The low-level perspective was very appealing to a couple of young naturalists and earned us unique sightings of otters at play, swimming caribou and flocking pelicans.

Since then, we've had many years of paddling together in which to contemplate just what makes kayaking such an extraordinary and different means of travel. Were it not for the marvelous invention of the kayak, we might never have enjoyed some of the adventures revealed in the photographs in this book. Exploring wild places by kayak from Greenland to Japan, from Lake Superior to Mexico, has given us a deeper sense of appreciation for this watery planet we live on.

When our daughter, Sila, was barely a month old, she was already spending many hours sleeping in canoes and kayaks, all the sensations of water and air filling her world. We felt we were her guides, letting nature be her teacher. By the time Sila was three, she intuitively knew a lot about being on and in the water. She was comfortable in any watercraft surfing waves, never minded getting doused unexpectedly, and keenly observant of the natural world. The innate sense of knowing by feeling is something best ingrained as children because as adults we have to work harder to achieve an instinctive response to our surroundings and the rhythms of the world around us.

Learning a sport such as kayaking is more than simply learning how to get in and do the forward stroke. It is a little like learning a new language. You first learn single words, then phrases and then whole stories. You have to learn to be fluent in the "language" of kayaking — the moves and materials, the forces, obstacles and opportunities — and especially because kayaking is something you do on the water, truly immersed in nature, you must learn to be adaptable to change. You can create in yourself the right instincts and responses by practice, by steeping yourself in knowledge, and by being open always to learning more. In this book, we demonstrate the strokes and the maneuvers of kayaking with step-by-step illustrated instructions. We look at the big picture too. We consider weather, wind and current, and how to respond to and prepare for all kinds of conditions, and navigate confidently in places where you have never been. Planning routes, reading charts and getting to and from the water safely are necessary elements of the experience; we've included what we think are helpful tips to help you on and off the water. And finally, we want to share our appreciation for the kayak itself, a craft that was at the center of a nomadic lifestyle for thousands of years along the Arctic Coast.

A number of years ago we were on the west coast of Greenland, paddling south from Nuuk. The gray-blue sea was oily smooth. A low, cool fog hung barely 20 feet above the water. Twice we had spotted whales, their dark sleek backs breaking the surface. Our bows cut a wake through the silence. We imagined ourselves back in a time when there were only kayaks, umiaks and dogsleds. Then we heard something. Stopping to listen, we realized it was voices. Two paddlers speaking in Greenlandic came out of the mist. They could have been ghosts of two Inuit hunters from long ago, so traditional were the shapes of their kayaks and the materials from which they were made. Grinning from ear to ear, they approached us. The fact that we did not have a shared language was of little concern. We were, by virtue of our kayaks, sharing common ground and had much to learn from each other.

In this book, we are first and foremost encouraging you — you and your partner, you and your children, you and your parents, you and your friends — to explore nature. Once you find comfort in this home of air, earth and water, you will no doubt be struck with the desire and confidence to explore it further. We hope you will find, as we have, that the kayak is an ideal vehicle to transport you to the mysteries and rewards of the natural world.

CHAPTER 2

THE KAYAK

MAKING DECISIONS ABOUT CHOOSING A KAYAK, whether it be to purchase your own or to use one provided by an outfitter on a guided excursion, begins with understanding the basics about design, materials, features and their purpose. The more informed you are, the more questions you can ask, and the more comfortable you are, the more fun you will have kayaking.

There are a few questions you can ask yourself when you are getting started kayaking, and they are worth reconsidering as your experience grows. You may not have the time or resources to venture out on a big adventure right now, but it is in having those dreams that you can plan and work toward acquiring the necessary skills. In fact, kayaking can open your eyes to extraordinary sights in familiar locales, things that have always been there but have gone unnoticed. As you look at photographs through a kayaker's eyes or read travel and adventure stories of spectacular journeys to exciting places you will see yourself being there. Consider where you want to be able to go in a kayak right now. Do you want to kayak and camp, or take daytrips only? If you are a birdwatcher, artist, photographer, fisher or skin diver, you will find kayaking is compatible with these and many other pursuits. Are you planning to kayak on the open ocean or other expansive water bodies, or will you be on sheltered waters? Is storage and transportation of a kayak an issue for you? Collapsible kayaks, renting a kayak, or joining a local canoe and kayak club are all very good options.

Learning from Others

Before you start planning your inaugural trip, and before you decide what kind of kayak and gear you will need, we recommend that you take a kayaking course.

It is really worthwhile to start out on the right foot with good technique. Not only will you not develop bad habits, you will not get frustrated and, more important, you will be less likely to get into dangerous situations. Instructional programs are available to suit every range of ability but the novice kayaker in particular will find the most offerings. There are many annual paddling symposiums that occur in on-water locations across North America. These are places to try out kayaks, meet fellow paddlers and get a taste of new coastlines, lakeshores and rivers. Although you can attend a short introductory session at a kayak symposium, consider taking at least a full one- or two-day course to cover the basic skills. You will increase your enjoyment on the water, learn about safety from experienced paddlers, and find answers to your many questions.

There are two main certifying bodies, the American Canoe and Kayak Association (the ACA), and the British Canoe Union (BCU). The ACA focuses a bit more on perfecting paddling skills and teaching methods, and the BCU (because of its open sea heritage) emphasizes capsize recovery skills and group leadership in a wide variety of sea conditions. As you progress in the sport, no matter how advanced a paddler you become, you can continue to be challenged to improve your skills.

You can also consider taking a guided excursion. There are innumerable attractive options, but keep in mind that a pleasure trip is not a substitute for an instructional course. A talented, skilled guide will assist you along the way, but the focus is on the sights and experiences, not on making you a better kayaker. Also, you would be wise to do some research into any guiding company before you sign on for a trip. Ask for references and talk with people who have traveled with them.

OPPOSITE Floating on Lake Superior feels like flying. The house-size boulders 20 feet beneath us seem close enough to touch.

BELOW A snug, comfortable fit helps you be at one with the kayak. With practice comes confidence; you will find your balance in conditions rough and calm.

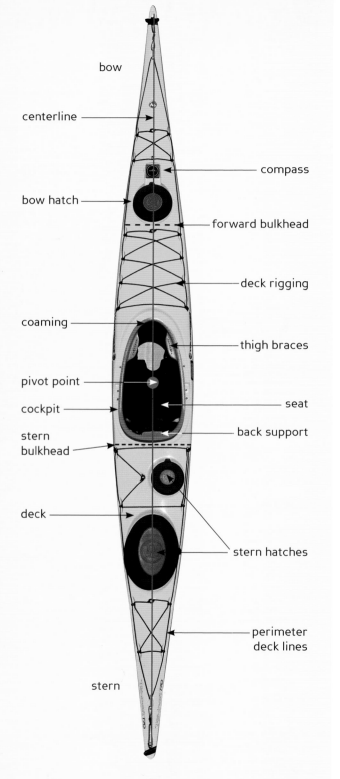

bow

centerline

compass

bow hatch

forward bulkhead

deck rigging

coaming

thigh braces

pivot point

seat

cockpit

back support

stern bulkhead

stern hatches

deck

perimeter deck lines

stern

A Kayaker's Vocabulary

You will find it useful to know the names of the parts of the kayak and the language of kayaking in general as you progress through this book. The skills have a language all their own that is best understood in the context of each section (for example, in capsize recoveries, strokes and maneuvers, navigation) and that language is further explained as needed.

CHINE is the curve of the kayak at the point where the sides meet the bottom. The sharpness of this curve influences secondary stability, as when the kayak is edged (tipped) to one side or the other. A hard-chine kayak has a square or angular profile between the bottom and sides, whereas a hull design that is rounded between the bottom and sides has a soft chine.

DECK PROFILE The shape, or profile, of the deck is viewed along the centerline of the kayak. It can be flat, gently cambered or decidedly peaked. The deck forward of the cockpit usually has more pronounced contours than the stern deck. The contour and volume of the kayak above the waterline affect the kayak's behavior, especially in wind. A flat forward deck profile presents less resistance to the wind but is generally a wetter ride in windy seas. A more voluminous, peaked deck can shed the waves, making for a drier ride, and it can also be more comfortable for larger paddlers.

FLARE is the progressive widening of the hull upward from the waterline; it serves to deflect water and increase stability and storage capacity. Adding flare in the bow increases buoyancy and makes for a drier ride when paddling into waves.

KEEL LINE is a line running from bow to stern along the centerline on the underside of the hull.

ROCKER is the degree of curvature along the keel line from bow to stern. The more rocker in the hull, the more the bow and stern ends are raised and kept from making contact with the water. The greater the rocker there is, the less resistance the ends provide to turning.

SHAPE A kayak sitting in the water leaves the impression of its shape, otherwise known as its footprint. A kayak's greatest width can be at its centerpoint (in a symmetrical hull), forward of center (fish-form) or aft of center (Swede-form). The shape — width, length and rocker — affects the kayak's efficiency in turning and in tracking.

SHEER is the longitudinal profile above the waterline from bow to stern as viewed from the side of the kayak. The sheer line of a kayak can be viewed along the top edge of the hull.

STABILITY A flat-bottomed kayak has primary stability because it feels stable when it is sitting flat on the water. But since water is not a stable platform like flat ground, a kayaker is more concerned with secondary stability, that is, the stability of the kayak when it is edged from side to side. The kayak's front-on profile best reveals the characteristics that affect stability: the hull shape, flare, the sharpness of the chines, the beam and the waterline beam.

TRACKING is the tendency of a boat to go in a straight line. If the kayak has a straight keel line, it is said to have good tracking ability. A hull shape for a touring kayak balances the attributes of tracking and rocker, that balance depending on which attribute is more greatly desired, the ability to turn quickly or to keep on course easily.

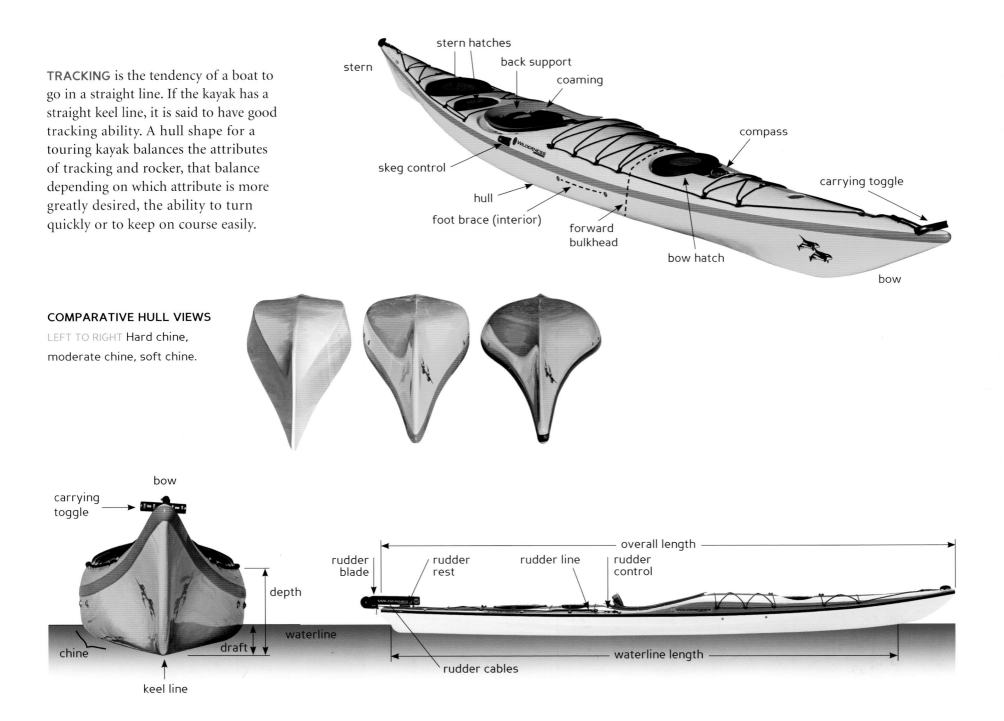

stern hatches

back support

stern

coaming

compass

skeg control

carrying toggle

hull

foot brace (interior)

forward bulkhead

bow hatch

bow

COMPARATIVE HULL VIEWS

LEFT TO RIGHT Hard chine, moderate chine, soft chine.

bow

carrying toggle

depth

waterline

chine

draft

keel line

rudder blade

rudder rest

rudder line

rudder control

overall length

rudder cables

waterline length

A Comparison of Kayak Shapes

Since the first kayaks, constructed of animals skins and thin wood frames, were made several thousand years ago, it is impossible to pinpoint exactly when and where they did appear. But we do know they were an integral part of people's lives from Greenland to the North Pacific. The detailed sketches and paintings of early Russian and European explorers provide a record both of the presence of kayaks in these coastal communities and of the intricate workmanship of those ancient watercraft. Designs and materials evolved depending on the conditions and needs of the people using them. Coastal people relied on the kayak to acquire the sea animals that provided food, fuel, clothing, shelter and tools. For thousands of years, all along the Arctic coast from the Bering Strait to Greenland, a low-volume, narrow, swift little craft would have been seen among the ice floes. The paddler, generally hunting walrus and seals, would have been a person of extraordinary skill and knowledge the likes of which do not exist today. On winter days when the kayaks are tucked in the barn, we delight in mulling over the maps and story books describing life among early Arctic hunting peoples. The fascination and respect for their lives grows as you yourself kayak. And the admiration and wonder with which you find yourself gazing down on your own kayak when you are out on the open water will never dull.

EXPEDITION TOURING

This 18-foot expedition touring kayak is fast, responsive and seaworthy. With sealed bulkheads and hatches fore and aft, there is plenty of storage space to carry gear for a multi-day or multi-week adventure. It is outfitted with a retractable skeg.

TOURING

This 16 1/2-foot sea kayak has a comforting stability and is responsive and seaworthy. It is outfitted with sealed hatches fore and aft, making it suitable for daytripping or multi-day tripping. It has a drop-down rudder.

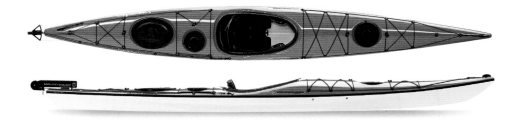

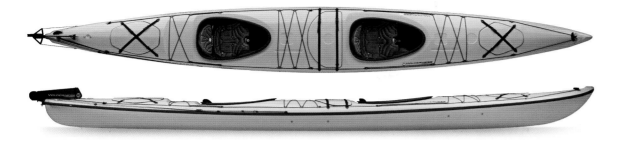

TANDEM TOURING

Tandem kayaks are stable and seaworthy. They carry a lot of gear and can generally be paddled faster than singles (as you have double the paddle power). They are great for two paddlers who want to paddle together but whose fitness and skill level is very different. These 20-foot-plus kayaks can also provide space for carrying small children or a dog in the center cockpit.

RECREATIONAL LIGHT TOURING

This 14 1/2-foot recreational kayak is perfect for a quiet afternoon on a gentle river or small lake. There is enough storage space for daytripping gear with sealed bulkheads in the bow and stern hatches.

SIT-ON-TOP

This 12-foot sit-on-top is a recreational kayak meant for use on small lakes, ponds, and marshes — in other words, calm, protected waters. It has a small waterproof hatch with enough room for daytripping gear. This kayak is quite maneuverable, and very easy to reenter if you capsize.

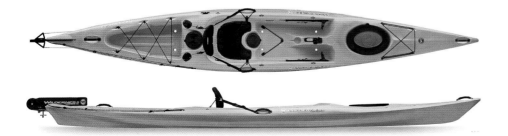

SPECIALIZED SIT-ON-TOP FOR FISHING

The extra length makes this 16-foot sit-on-top a sportier model, more for performance paddling. This particular one has been outfitted for kayak fishing, a very popular pursuit.

Kayak Materials

Kayaks are made of a variety of materials. The two yellow kayaks pictured here are of composite construction, meaning that layers of cloth have been hardened to a rigid shape in a two-part, top and bottom mold with a quick-curing resin. Kayaks such as the fiberglass model in the foreground are widely available, repairable in the field and less expensive than a comparable kayak made of Kevlar. The tandem kayak (in the background) is made of the lighter, stronger, more expensive fabric called Kevlar. Given the size of the kayak, the extra cost is well repaid in reduced back and muscle strain every time you lift it. The orange kayak is a rotomolded polyethylene model, making it highly durable, abrasion resistant and much less costly than a comparable composite hull. It is a popular choice for outfitters and families for both of these reasons. The white kayak is one that we made (see Chapter 15, Building Your Own Kayak). It is constructed of lightweight plywood with a fiberglass epoxy coating. Those who want to build their own kayak may consider other construction methods, including skin-on-frame, which is a treated fabric stretched over a wood frame, or a beautiful, all-wood cedar-strip kayak. Also see folding kayaks in Chapter 13, Planning Your Own Adventure, for a look at a high-tech kayak that combines the ancient method of skin-on-frame with modern materials.

FOREGROUND TO BACKGROUND Fiberglass, plastic, wood covered with a layer of fiberglass, Kevlar.

The Cockpit and How to Sit in a Kayak

The cockpit area of a kayak should fit you like a good shoe fits your foot. It has to feel snug and comfortable, without chafing or pinching. Think of wearing your kayak rather than sitting in it. Only with correct seat, hip, thigh, knee and foot contact will you have proper boat control and also avoid common kayak ailments, in particular, lower back strain. Your bottom should fit the seat snugly but not tightly. An adjustable back support will give you the proper lower-back support, enabling an upright posture for torso rotation.

Stretch your legs out then draw them back up a bit so they are bent into a sort of diamond shape with your knees splayed out and your heels pointed toward the centerline of the kayak. The balls of your feet should rest comfortably on the foot braces and your knees and thighs should be well anchored under the cockpit coaming and thigh braces.

A good commercial seat such as this one has an adjustable back support, seat and hip pads and padded thigh braces. This seat offers the additional support of an adjustment under the thighs.

Sit in the kayak with good posture; adjust the seat's back support if necessary. Your legs form a relaxed diamond shape with your heels turned toward the centerline and your knees and thighs pressing against the thigh braces. Adjust your foot braces so that the balls of your feet rest easily against them.

This homemade seat meets the same needs of fit and comfort by using closed-cell foam carved to customize a seat and thigh braces. We installed an adjustable back band.

Bulkheads and Hatches

Modern touring kayaks often have sealed bulkheads (internal walls) separating the cockpit area from the bow and stern chambers where you store your gear. These chambers also act as essential flotation for the kayak in the event of a capsize. There are hatch covers on the deck that allow entry into these storage areas. The method used to seal the cover needs to be waterproof. Some kayaks use a rubber lid; these work well on small openings. Others use a neoprene cover, which is then covered with the solid hatch cover. The larger the hatch opening, the easier it is to access gear, but the harder it is to seal well. More sophisticated sealing methods include a neoprene gasket pressed snugly into place by the hard-shell hatch cover.

Special crisscross webbing systems combined with cam-lock buckles keep these lids pressed against the gasket to prevent leakage.

If you do not have sealed bulkheads, you must install inflated flotation bags at the bow and stern to displace water in the event of a capsize. In this situation, your gear must be stored in dry bags. However we highly advise packing with dry bags even for sealed compartments. Under the duress conditions of a capsize, when the hatches may go underwater, gaskets can fail, hatch covers can come loose and condensation may occur. It is quite discouraging to open your hatch at day's end to discover a soggy sleeping bag, sopping-wet clothing and or unusable food.

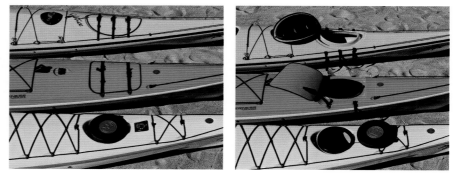

STERN HATCHES The yellow kayak in the foreground makes use of rubber covers both bow and stern to seal the hatches. There is a second small stern hatch behind the cockpit on this kayak that is used as waterproof storage for items needed during the day such as extra clothing, lunch and snacks. The orange kayak employs a neoprene cover to create a waterproof seal, which is then covered with a hard-shell lid secured with straps fastened with Fastex buckles. The gold kayak uses hard-shell lids, each with an integral gasket. The stern hatches have larger openings, making them ideal for longer, bulkier items such as sleeping pads, cooking pots and tents.

BOW HATCHES The bow hatches have smaller openings, so are best for shorter, more compact items. The bow hatch takes more of the brunt of the waves. The gold kayak in the background employs cam-lock buckles to increase the pressure on the seal once the lid is secured with the straps.

Most items are best stored safely in a dry hatch until you reach shore. But some items such as a pump and a paddle float are good to have at the ready, and, of course, a map is only useful when it is out on the deck ready to read.

Rudders and Skegs

Many kayaks have either a foot-controlled rudder or a retractable skeg. Both are designed to enhance the tracking ability of the kayak. The rudder also allows you to steer the kayak with your feet: push on the right foot brace and you will veer right; push left and you go left. Both the rudder and skeg are each easily deployed with one hand, using a mechanism located on the deck near the cockpit. The control cable operating the rudder is usually spring-loaded so that the rudder can lift up and over obstructions beneath the surface. While the rudder is either in or out of the water, the skeg can be dropped by a slide adjustment to varying levels depending on the tracking assistance needed. A word of caution: Although they are very useful in traveling a straight course on windy days with quartering seas, rudders and skegs are not a substitute for good paddling technique. They are handy for those times when you want to put your paddle down and use your binoculars or camera and still stay on course. The rudder is especially helpful in this case, as you can steer with your feet. And in awkward paddling conditions, a tandem kayak is much easier to keep on track with a rudder. We think rudders and skegs are wonderful tools; however, beginners are wise to use them sparingly. Paddling strokes and an innate sense of balance need to be honed in all conditions, as these aids can fail, and when they do, you will want to know that you can get to where you are going without them.

You can vary the amount of skeg in the water but you can't maneuver it from side to side. The foot braces in this kayak are locked into one position, providing constant bracing, but they are not involved in the steering process.

When the skeg is up, it retracts into a skeg box molded into the hull. The groove should be checked regularly to make sure it is free of sand and stones that would prevent the skeg from dropping down.

A foot-operated rudder is controlled by rudder cables that run back to either side of the rudder. The kayaker can control raising or lowering the rudder with one hand using a mechanism located on the deck near the cockpit. Once down, the rudder provides not only tracking ability, but strong turning ability, too. Push with your left foot and turn left. Push right, turn right.

A rudder that lifts right up and over the stern to land in a rudder rest on the back deck is preferable to one that merely clears the water. The rudder is safely stored and its side-to-side movement is curtailed, transforming the steering foot braces into fixed foot braces. When transporting this kayak on a vehicle, use the elastic strap to hold the rudder in place.

CHAPTER 3

THE OUTFIT

PERUSE ANY PADDLING CATALOG and you will be amazed at the number and variety of products that are available for kayaking. You may feel overwhelmed by the choice or indeed the feeling that you won't be able to get into this sport because you simply can't afford all the gear. First off, know that the best of gear won't ever replace a person's skill, experience and judgment, hence the wisdom in getting good instruction. However, good equipment can mean the difference between comfort and great discomfort. Certain equipment is a necessity; you can't paddle a kayak without a paddle. Certain equipment is required by regulation for safety, such as your PFD (personal flotation device). For some equipment, such as towing systems and signaling devices, you will need instruction before you can use them anyway. If you are kayaking on your lake at the cottage, you don't really need a VHF radio. Consider what kind of paddling you are going to be doing and what gear is going to be necessary for your experience.

The Lake Superior National Marine Conservation Area is a kayaking mecca with its countless islands, small coves, deep bays and sheer cliffs.

The Paddle

Both the kayak and the paddle can be thought of as extensions of your body, connecting you intimately with the water. We've already discussed how choosing the right kayak is key. In the same way, your comfort and enjoyment of kayaking will be helped immeasurably by choosing the paddle that is right for you. Every time you go kayaking you will be holding and lifting this tool. Its length, weight, blade shape, materials and balance need to satisfy you.

Paddle Types and Sizing

Paddles are made of wood, fiberglass, aluminum, plastic, Kevlar, graphite and various combinations of these materials. With the exception of some of the solid wood paddles shown here, most kayak paddles are of a two-piece take-apart design, which is an advantage when it comes to transporting the paddle, storing it and fastening an extra one to your deck. While a fiberglass shaft with plastic blades makes for a good general-purpose paddle, we appreciate the joy of touring with a paddle that is either featherlight graphite or beautiful wood. When it comes to tradition and paddling a Greenland kayak, we enjoy using our handmade wooden paddles. The beauty of the grain and the colors, natural buoyancy, and warmth for your hands makes them very pleasing in the age of synthetics. Today, paddle manufacturers are combining different materials to acquire excellent compromises in durability and price. The synthetics combine fiberglass, carbon fiber or Kevlar for the blades, and fiberglass, graphite or aluminum for the shafts. One of the paddle types we use has a crank shaft that is supposed to make more ergonomic sense for your wrists. Although we have never warmed to their feel, many people swear by them.

When you hold a paddle, it should have a balanced feeling. The only thing more important than the feel of the paddle is the comfort of the kayak. Things that are initially a little bothersome are guaranteed to drive you crazy over the long haul. So take your time choosing and buy the best you can afford.

The overall length of your paddle is determined by your kayak's beam, your height and the blade design as well as the kind of paddling you are interested in. Overall lengths range from 87 to 102 inches (210–260 cm). At 5 feet, 4 inches, I generally paddle with a 220 cm paddle and Gary, at 6 feet, prefers a 230 cm paddle.

The ferrule on these take-apart paddles is a very strong union of the two halves. There are adjustment holes to give you either a feathered or unfeathered paddle, and to make the twist either left- or right-handed. Inspect and wipe the ferrule clean regularly to prevent sand-salt residue or any fine debris from seizing it up.

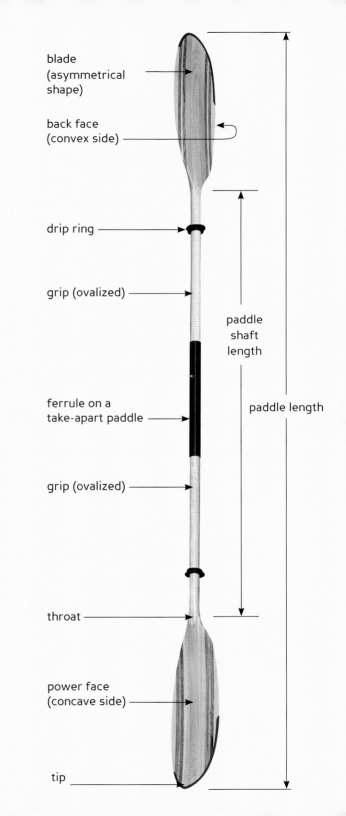

blade (asymmetrical shape)

back face (convex side)

drip ring

grip (ovalized)

paddle shaft length

ferrule on a take-apart paddle

paddle length

grip (ovalized)

throat

power face (concave side)

tip

PADDLE TYPES AND MATERIALS

Paddles are made from a variety of materials and combinations thereof. Paddle types from left to right:

1. Child's take-apart carbon-fiber shaft with carbon-reinforced thermoplastic blades,
2. Child's solid wood shaft with unfeathered blades,
3. Child's solid wood Greenland or Inuit,
4. Take-apart with wood laminated blades and stainless-steel ferrule,
5. Take-apart with wood/fiberglass laminated blades and carbon-fiber ferrule,
6. Solid wood Greenlandic or Inuit,
7. Fiberglass shaft with narrow fiberglass-reinforced thermoplastic blades,
8. Carbon-fiber shaft with wider carbon-reinforced thermoplastic blades,
9. Take-apart with carbon-fiber crankshaft and narrow touring blades,
10. Take-apart carbon-fiber shaft with narrow touring blades,
11. Take-apart carbon-fiber shaft with wide blades.

Paddle blades come in many shapes. They are symmetrical, asymmetrical, short and wide, or long and narrow. If you are touring, a narrower, elongated asymmetrical blade is most compatible for the slower paddling cadence and lower shaft angle. Those who are paddling vigorously in surf and waves, needing short bursts of power with a more vertical shaft angle, will likely find a wider blade advantageous. In contrast, the typical Greenland paddle shown is altogether quite different. It was constructed from one piece of wood with very narrow (less than 4 inches, or 10 cm) blades and the shaft, or loom, is in one piece.

Obviously no single paddle will be perfect for every circumstance. Finally, providing a child with a properly sized and proportioned paddle makes it more enjoyable and enables him or her to better emulate your strokes and maneuvers.

FEATHERED OR UNFEATHERED BLADES

The blades on an unfeathered paddle are on the same plane, whereas a feathered paddle has offset blades that range between 45 to 75 degrees. With an unfeathered paddle, when you take a stroke on one side, the recovering blade on the opposite side of the kayak is perpendicular to the surface of the water. (If you ever experience the common ailment of wrist strain while kayaking, using an unfeathered paddle helps you to keep your forearm and wrist aligned.) The advantage of a feathered paddle is most noticeable in the recovery part of the forward stroke in a headwind. The blade is slicing forward relatively horizontal to the water surface thereby offering less resistance to the wind. For more about this, turn to the forward stroke in Chapter 8, Strokes and Maneuvers.

Most touring paddles come as two-piece designs joined by a ferrule. There are different points of adjustment at the ferrule, which means you can adjust this offset of the blades to be left, right or unfeathered. Most of us have a natural tendency to prefer a right or left twist to the blades; generally, right-handed people like the blade twisted to the right. (This means that your right hand will be your control hand and will not let go of the paddle shaft, while your left hand will hold the shaft loosely so that it twists without your left wrist bending.) To adjust the offset, place the paddle upright in front of you. With the power face of the lower blade facing toward you, twist the upper half of the paddle shaft so that the power face is aiming to the right. (Left-handers should twist the upper half of the paddle so that the power face is aiming left.) Whatever you decide on, stick with it so that you always know where your blades are when you need to put in a quick brace.

Paddles with crank shafts and wing-shaped blades are meant to ease strain on a paddler's joints, and increase efficiency and paddling performance. Greenland-style paddles are unfeathered, and their long, narrow blades do not catch the wind.

FEATHERED BLADES

UNFEATHERED BLADES

HOW TO HOLD THE PADDLE

Hold your paddle out in front of you with your hands equidistant from the center of the shaft and a little more than shoulder width apart. Hold the paddle with a relaxed grip. Keep your wrist aligned with your forearm to prevent wrist strain.

Personal Flotation Device

A PFD (personal flotation device) or life vest is essential and, in most jurisdictions, legally required. Start by choosing one that is Coast Guard approved and comfortable for you to wear all the time with a range of clothing. (A PFD is hard to put on in the water, which is just where you need it. People who die from drowning nearly always are not wearing a PFD.) A wide selection of styles are available in a soft, contoured fit with front, side and over-the-head entry options. For kayaking, you are looking for a vest that is cut short so it won't ride up around your ears when you are seated in your kayak. When selecting a PFD, try it on. Cinch up the straps so it is snug. Sit down as if you are in a kayak and pretend you are paddling to see if there is any chafing under the arms or other discomfort. Have someone haul up on the shoulder straps. The vest should stay low on your body. For safety sake, bright colors are important so that you can be seen from a distance. Reflective tape on the vest makes you highly visible. Attach a pea-less safety whistle to your jacket, either on the zipper pull, the shoulder strap or a chest pocket. There are various styles of PFDs such as the one illustrated here that feature pockets (which are handy for an energy bar, compass, rescue sling, etc.). We have found an integral harness with towline system extremely useful and effective, but some instruction and practice are required so that you know how to use this equipment properly.

OPPOSITE Armed with the proper skills, experience and equipment, you can tackle big surf.

RIGHT The front view of this PFD reveals a quick-release harness with the red ball on the buckle, a handy knife to cut free from a rope entanglement, a pigtail towline attached to the front pocket with a corrosion-resistant carabiner, and a pea-less whistle fastened to the zipper pull.

The Sprayskirt

The sprayskirt allows you to stay dry inside your kayak by sealing off the cockpit. It attaches around your waist, and the lower edge of the skirt is fastened around the cockpit coaming. In rough and cold weather, the sprayskirt is necessary for both comfort and safety. It is the sprayskirt that allows you to roll your kayak without getting any water in the cockpit. Sprayskirts are made from nylon and or neoprene. Nylon sprayskirts are flexible, comfortable and easy to put on. Neoprene sprayskirts will, however, stay on much more reliably in rough conditions. There are also hybrids that have a neoprene skirt and a nylon waist tunnel. Nylon skirts are best suspended with shoulder straps. Sprayskirts need to be worn under your PFD so that the waist tunnel makes the best seal around your waist, otherwise water will enter your kayak at this point. Keep in mind that the waist tunnel may need to be large enough to fit around some extra layers of clothing. Sprayskirts come sized for two measures — the cockpit's rim circumference and the paddler's waist size. Make sure you have the right one.

ATTACHING THE SPRAYSKIRT

The skirt needs to fit around the kayak coaming relatively snugly or it will come off, defeating its sole purpose. This is the one thing that makes many first-time paddlers nervous — the idea of sealing yourself into the kayak and, should you tip, the feeling that you will not be able to get out of the kayak. With a little practice, these fears will be banished. You will actually fall out of the kayak quite easily. Attaching the sprayskirt to the cockpit can be a frustrating business for the uninitiated, especially if it is a neoprene one. The trick is to start at the back. Sit up straight, reach back and tuck the edge of the skirt under the coaming. Keep working it forward with one hand on either side until you reach a point by your hips. Pin it down with your forearms and stretch it out over the front of the coaming. Make sure the grab loop stays on the outside of the skirt. Now the sides of the skirt can easily be worked over the

DIFFERENT TYPES OF SPRAYSKIRTS

Nylon sprayskirt with adjustable waist and shoulder straps.

Neoprene sprayskirt with adjustable waist.

Hybrid sprayskirt combining a nylon waist tunnel with shoulder straps, adjustable waist, and a neoprene skirt with handy attachment points.

coaming. A neoprene skirt can be made a bit more flexible by wetting it down, but if it is just impossible to get on, then it will be just as impossible to get it off. You need to find one that fits your cockpit properly.

A WORD ABOUT THE GRAB LOOP

Make sure that your grab loop is securely fastened to the sprayskirt, and that once you have the sprayskirt on, the loop is on the outside where you can reach it. The grab loop needs to be substantial enough to hang on to even with wet, cold, glove-covered hands.

1 Sit up straight, reach back and tuck the edge of the sprayskirt around the coaming.

2 Keep working it forward with one hand on either side of the skirt until you reach a point at your hips.

3 Pin the skirt down with your forearms.

4 Stretch the front of the skirt over the front of the coaming. Now the sides of the skirt can easily be worked over the coaming.

5 Make sure the grab loop stays on the outside of the skirt.

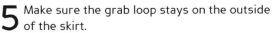

Dressing for Kayaking

As a paddler, your first concern is to protect yourself from the elements of wind, water, sun, cold and heat. When you are suitably and comfortably dressed, you can enjoy the weather, no matter what it brings. Let's start with the easiest scenario.

WARM AIR, WARM WATER

The greatest danger in such weather is getting burned from the sun, and becoming dehydrated. Wear a wide-brim hat that shades your head and neck, sunglasses with full ultraviolet protection, and loose-fitting, quick-dry, light-colored clothing. Cotton feels cool in the hot weather and, if you dampen it, dries slowly drawing heat from your body. I like to soak a cotton bandana and wrap it around my neck. River sandals or water shoes should be worn to protect your feet when you are out of the kayak.

Apply sunscreen to protect exposed skin, especially in the midday hours when the sun is most intense. This is especially important for children and people with sensitive, easy-to-burn skin.

Your body depends on hydration to keep cool and warm, so drink plenty of water throughout the day. If you feel thirsty, you are already dehydrated. Keep extra water bottles handy and stored out of the sun. Hydration backpacks have become a popular way of staying hydrated in many outdoor pursuits. You wear the water on your back and suck it from a little hose that comes over your shoulder.

WARM AIR, COLD WATER

We have all had the experience of setting off on a trip when the day is warm and sunny and it later turns cold and wet. We aren't prepared because the weather, when we left, didn't prompt our senses. Unless we have a checklist, important items such as a hat and foul-weather gear are easily forgotten.

Dressing for immersion is the easiest and safest rule to live by in kayaking when the water is cold. No matter how warm the air temperature, you need to be prepared for a capsize. Since cold-water immersion is the primary factor in kayaker deaths (and is almost always preventable), it is advisable to wear a sleeveless wetsuit in such conditions. These thin neoprene suits available with wide-cut armholes specifically for paddling come in either full or short-leg design. These suits known as a Farmer Johns (or Janes) will protect the core of your body from the cold. Also choose fabrics that are quick drying. Synthetic underwear worn as a base layer is ideal as it wicks any moisture away from your body. Several light layers are preferable to one heavy layer. Pulling on a paddling jacket can be just the ticket on a windy day, cutting heat loss considerably. However, choose one that works best for you. One with latex gaskets and neck will keep the water out in the event of a capsize, but you can also get too hot. Don't forget your wide-brimmed hat and sunglasses. Drink plenty of filtered fresh water. Just remember it is easier to get cooled down than warmed up.

COLD AIR, COLD WATER

Dress for immersion. It is so much easier to dress for cold water when it is already a cold, wet day. Both wetsuits and drysuits work well in these conditions. They will protect your body from the elements above and below the surface. When I was young, I did a lot of scuba diving even under the ice in the winter wearing a ¼-inch wetsuit. The first rush of cold water was shocking, but once this thin layer of water warmed against my skin, it was reasonably comfortable for an hour or so afterward even in submersed conditions. As kayakers we are generally not immersed to this degree unless we are practicing capsize recoveries and rescues. However, if you are playing in surf, where you can spend a lot of time getting drenched, there is nothing so comfortable as a drysuit. If you are an avid paddler and wish to expand your paddling season and extend your paddling destination range into colder regions, you will find a drysuit well worth the price. One with a breathable, waterproof membrane is the best choice for comfort. Choose insulating footwear such as neoprene booties. Synthetic underwear beneath the drysuit is usually all that is needed but you can add a lightweight fleece if the conditions warrant it. Remember you are also wearing a PFD vest that provides a certain amount of core protection from the cold as well. On a day where both the air and water are chilling, there is little room for error if you are not dressed for immersion. No matter how skilled and strong you are as a paddler and a swimmer, you are no match for the cold. Dress for a capsize.

PROTECTING YOUR HEAD AND HANDS

You lose half your heat from your head so it goes without saying that you need to put a lid on it. If you capsize in very cold water, an ice-cream headache can be avoided if you are wearing a neoprene beanie. A fleece skull cap is comfortable under a hood. In wet and windy weather, you will need something to keep your hands from going numb. Neoprene gloves and mitts work for many people but I like keeping my hands on the paddle shaft. Pogies are the answer. They attach to your paddle shaft with Velcro. You can hold the paddle with bare hands yet your hands are protected from the elements, and you can easily slip your hands in and out of them.

TIP BURPING THE DRYSUIT
For safety sake, before getting in your kayak, squeeze trapped air from your drysuit. Walk into the water up to your chest. Pull the gasket away from your neck and the air trapped in the suit will rush out, causing the suit to compress around you. The same thing can be accomplished simply by scrunching down into a tight crouch and releasing the air through the neck gasket.

Footwear

Shown here are some of our favorite choices for footwear. The knee-high mukluks are truly superb on a northern expedition or on any cold, wet paddling day. Your feet will stay warm and dry. When the weather is not so extreme, neoprene wetsuit boots provide warmth and ankle protection. Make sure they have a good foot bed for walking on rock or seashore. Neoprene socks add warmth to a pair of river sandals. There is a great variety of lightweight water shoes for hot weather, though you should try them in a paddling position to make sure nothing chafes or binds. Many are now designed to protect your toes and stay on your feet while swimming.

The idea of going barefoot may appeal but, considering all the possible things you might cut your feet on while out of your kayak, it is not at all wise. Depending on the terrain, weather and length of your trip, you have plenty of choices in footwear.

Hypothermia

As warm-blooded mammals, humans have a normal core temperature of around 98.6 degrees Fahrenheit (37° C). When this temperature drops, the body becomes hypothermic. As blood leaves the extremities of the hands and feet to protect the vital organs, the body begins shivering. This early stage of hypothermia will be closely followed or accompanied by the following symptoms: loss of manual dexterity, clumsiness, lethargy, blue lips and uncontrolled shivering. Since being wet draws your body heat away faster than the air, you can become hypothermic by paddling in a cold rain without the proper clothing to keep you dry. If you tip your kayak and find yourself immersed in 50° F (10° C) water, you have about 15 minutes in which you can accomplish something like getting back in the kayak. Within an hour, you will most likely be unconscious if not already drowned. Immersion in 40° F (5° C) without adequate protection means you have little more than 5 minutes before you are helpless and 15 minutes before you succumb.

Hypothermia is a serious matter that all paddlers need to be able to recognize in themselves and others around them. Doing something about it in the early stages is the best way to avoid the compounding difficulties. (When a mildly hypothermic paddler who has become lethargic and clumsy tips over, the symptoms suddenly accelerate. Even an experienced paddler will find it a great physical effort to get back in the kayak.) To avoid this, it is important to insist on getting yourself or any other person dry and warm immediately following the onset of hypothermic symptoms. Change into dry clothes with lots of insulation and protection from wind and rain, and remember to don a warm hat. The victim needs a warm drink (non-alcoholic) and something to eat. Vigorous exercise also helps.

Dressing appropriately for the water temperature is the key way to avoiding hypothermia in the first place.

Hyperthermia

The opposite of hypothermia is hyperthermia — heat exhaustion — when the core body temperature goes up because it cannot cool itself. A person suffering from heat exhaustion is usually flushed, sweating profusely, and often feeling dizzy. If left untreated, this will lead to a serious medical emergency called heat stroke in which the body core temperature continues to rise uncontrollably.

Drinking lots of water throughout the day is the key to preventing hyperthermia. Wearing a wide-brimmed hat, sunglasses and light clothing that protects you from the sun is also very important.

Caring for Your Equipment

We live in a 19th-century farmhouse. On the property there is a barn and a two-storey shed. Where once dairy cattle and work horses filled the space, our livestock now consists of a herd of canoes and kayaks. We are lucky to have a place where we can store our kayaks and our paddling gear out of the direct sunlight, extreme heat and moisture, as these three things are most damaging to your equipment. Keeping your gear undercover will greatly prolong its life. You can store a kayak on a rack outside as long as it is beneath an overhanging roof and protected from the elements. Do not store your kayak on a rack in direct sunlight covered with black plastic. Store your kayak either on its side or supported at the bulkheads. We have often suspended our kayaks from garage rafters using wide webbing as a cradle. Kayaks can deform, especially polyethylene ones, if they are simply suspended from their grab loops or the hull is left resting flat on narrow supports. We use cockpit covers to keep out unwanted winter guests. If you paddle on saltwater, you need to wash everything thoroughly on a regular basis.

The special clothing you purchase for paddling such as drysuits and wetsuits, paddling jackets, PFDs, pogies, helmets, booties and sprayskirts are an investment that if taken good care of will last you many years. If you paddle on the ocean, thoroughly wash salt out after every trip. Turn garments inside out to dry out completely, otherwise mildew will quickly begin to rot the fabric. Hang neoprene and drysuits up in a cupboard to avoid permanent creasing that results from long-term storage stuffed in a bag or drawer. Ultraviolet degradation will happen over time, so keep your equipment stored out of the sunlight.

If you check your equipment regularly, attend to minor repairs in a timely way, and provide proper storage in the off-season, you can avoid most equipment failures while out on the water.

RIGHT Choosing what to wear paddling among icebergs can be a dilemma on a day when the temperature is warm enough for T-shirts. A Farmer John (or Jane) wetsuit that insulates your torso is the best solution.

CHAPTER 4

BALANCING THE BODY

I F WE APPROACHED KAYAKING AS A COMPETITIVE SPORT, then our journeys would represent weeks and months of honing skills, developing endurance and building strength. We admire dedication to perfection in any pursuit; after all, it is within the competitive world that new ideas emerge and, for example, more efficient paddling techniques evolve. Those techniques developed by the competitive kayaker can be applied to recreational paddling.

If you have ever watched the lithe, fluid movements of a wolf as compared to those of a domestic dog, you can appreciate the beauty of efficiency in motion. People who paddled kayaks long ago probably paddled with the same finesse that today's athletes strive for, because for them kayaking was not a matter of winning, but more a matter of survival. Kayaking may not be a matter of survival for us, but paddling efficiently has many benefits. Kayaking efficiently is good for your body. It means less stress and strain on joints and small muscles because the effort is spread out over your whole body. Kayaking efficiently means going farther faster, with less effort.

OPPOSITE Sometimes the wind requires us to stay safely onshore. When we do, there is always much to enjoy, whether it be a walk or just sitting and observing the water.

RIGHT A beaver pond or small creek near home may not occur at first as a place to paddle your kayak, but such locations can become havens in which we find a healthy balance in our busy lives.

All our lives in every season we have enjoyed a variety of physical pursuits. We can't help but compare kayaking to telemark skiing, canoeing and bicycling. In all these activities, your body's balance point is your belly button. Keep your body centered over this point and you will be balanced. Efficient technique, be it in paddling or otherwise, has far more to do with balancing the body — maintaining your equilibrium with control and finesse — than with brute strength.

Years ago we adopted yoga and its fluid pattern of postures, attention to breathing and mind-relaxing meditation as a complement to our various outdoor pursuits. We have found that by executing a series of motions based on the natural movements of the spine, overall flexibility and balance are greatly improved.

Yoga postures are body positions that are performed in a balanced sequence, each in a static and dynamic phase. Each posture is held for a short time in a relaxed but attentive manner. While in the motionless phase, pay attention to your stretched muscles and your breathing. The dynamic phase involves moving fluidly from one posture to another. Breathe slowly, deeply and naturally. Inhale while lifting your legs, arms, and torso, and exhale when lowering them.

Yoga fosters a supple, flexible body. Muscles and tendons that are limber are less subject to injury. The Twist posture, as you will see, is excellent for working on the torso rotation discussed throughout Chapter 8, Strokes and Maneuvers. As you study the photos here, keep in mind that the postures should be performed at your own level of flexibility. You may not be able to get your toes anywhere near the ground in the Full Plow, or your head to your knees in the Forward Bend. What matters is that you do what you can using your inhalations and exhalations to relax into the position a little more each time you do it. By learning to control our breathing, we can control our bodies in magic ways. A quiet mind is an open

1 SITTING POSTURE Fold your legs beneath your bottom with the soles of your feet turned up and heels out. Place hands on thighs keeping back, neck and head straight.

and aware mind. You gain the greatest benefit from yoga in this state. Yoga also helps visualization, an awake dreaming state in which we see and feel ourselves accomplishing something before we physically do it. Visualize yourself paddling with grace, edging with abandon and rolling without hesitation and, with practice, you will be successful. In addition to the yoga postures, we have shown a couple of specific stretches useful for kayaking to loosen your shoulders and give your hamstrings an extra stretch.

2 Lie on your stomach with head turned to one side, legs relaxed, heels splayed outward and arms resting by sides. Inhale and exhale deeply, feeling the ground beneath you.

3 **COBRA POSTURE** Lie on your stomach, legs together, palms on the ground with fingertips at shoulders. Tuck elbows in. Raise head slowly, eyes to the sky. Your head, chest and abdomen are raised, but your belly button stays touching the ground.

4 **FULL LOCUST** Lying on your stomach, place chin on ground, arms by sides, legs together. Slowly and smoothly raise legs and chest from the ground while inhaling. Hold your breath and the posture, then exhale while lowering legs to the ground.

5 **FULL BOW** Lie flat on your stomach, legs spread a little, arms at sides with chin on ground. Grasp ankles with hands and slowly raise head from ground, looking skyward. Raise thighs from ground by pressing feet against hands. Hold, then lower smoothly.

6 **HALF PLOW** Lie on your back, legs together, knees straight. Raise legs together on inhalation. Keep chin tucked in so neck and head are pressed to the ground and shoulders are relaxed.

7 **FULL PLOW** This begins with the half plow. From the vertical leg position, lower legs back over head. Concentrate on your spine, lower vertebra by vertebra to the ground. Inhale and then exhale drawing your knees to your forehead and toes to the ground.

8 RECOVERY FROM FULL OR HALF PLOW Slowly return legs to the upright position. Inhale then exhale as you lower your legs in a controlled way to the ground.

9 BUTTOCKS STRETCH, RIGHT SIDE Lie on your back. Pull your knees to your chest. Cross your right leg over your left. With your fingers interlocked, clasp your left leg and gently squeeze your leg toward your chest, feeling the stretch in your right buttock.

BUTTOCKS STRETCH, LEFT SIDE Same as number 9 only pass the left leg over the right. Clasp the right leg and feel the stretch in the left buttock.

11 WHEEL POSTURE Stand straight, shoulders back and down, feet facing forward. Raise left arm until it is level with your shoulder. Turn palm up, raising arm to ear. Bend upper body from the waist, stretching on left and kinking on right. Repeat on other side.

12 TRIANGLE POSTURE STAGE 1 Take a wide stance with feet forward. Extend arms sideways in line with you shoulders. Turn left foot 45 degrees, then turn your body to left side and bend from waist, bringing your right hand to your left foot.

STAGE 2 With your left arm stretched up, turn head to look into left palm. Maintaining twist, raise your body then turn forward. Repeat steps on other side.

10 **FORWARD BEND STAGE 1** Stand erect with toes forward, feet together and weight equally distributed. Knees are relaxed with shoulders back and down. Slowly raise straight arms. Bend back from the waist, squeezing the buttocks.

STAGE 2 Lean forward from the lower spine, with your back straight, reaching out with straight arms and outstretched fingertips. Lead with your chin.

STAGE 3 Reach forward until bend is complete. Arms, shoulders, neck and head hang totally relaxed. Holding legs, gently encourage head to knees at each breath. Straighten, unfurling like a fern.

13 **BOAT POSTURE** With legs outstretched, arms at sides and palms on ground, slowly raise legs together. Balance on buttocks, then raise hands, reaching out toward your knees. Breathe. Lower legs and straighten back while exhaling.

14 **TWIST POSTURE** Place your right foot on the outside of the left knee. Place right arm with straight elbow behind your back, palm flat and fingers facing back. Reach left arm across bent right leg. Keep arm straight with left elbow pressed against right thigh. Straighten back and twist spine, looking over right shoulder. Repeat on other side.

15 **HAMSTRING AND ANKLE STRETCH** Reach forward keeping legs straight. Hold toes and inhale. As you exhale, bring your chest to your knees. Breathe deeply and release slowly.

16 WARRIOR POSTURE STAGE 1 Fold legs beneath buttocks. Rest buttocks on insteps. With back, neck and head straight, bring both arms behind you, grasping the right wrist with the thumb and index finger of the left hand.

STAGE 2 Leading with your chin, bend forward until your forehead touches the ground. Keep your buttocks resting on your insteps, hands still clasped behind you. Let your elbows relax. Return to upright by unfurling your spine.

17 TOTAL RELAXATION Lie on your back, palms up, legs outstretched, feet splayed outward, and eyes half closed. Visualize each part of your body relaxing bit by bit, working up from the toes. Relax completely — but without falling asleep.

19 THE PADDLE TWIST STAGE 1 With the paddle over your head. Hold the shaft at the throat of each blade.

STAGE 2 Drop the left hand and raise the right arm. Keep your body straight, feeling the stretch in your right shoulder and down your right side.

STAGE 3 Drop the right hand behind your back so that the shaft is horizontal to the ground. Both hands are still on the shaft.

18 SIDE STRETCH STAGE 1 Hold the paddle overhead with hands gripping the shaft lightly at the throat of each blade.

STAGE 2 Drop the left hand down, feeling the right arm being drawn over the head. Gently pull down with your left hand, continuing to feel the stretch up the whole right side of the body as it bends sideways, not forward or backward.

STAGE 3 Pull the right hand back down, feeling the left side rising until your paddle is in an overhead position. Again, feel the sideways stretch, being careful not to bend forward or backward.

STAGE 4 Now raise the left hand, feeling the stretch in the left shoulder and up the left side of your body.

STAGE 5 Now drop the right hand forward so that the paddle is parallel to the ground and in front of your body. Do this motion one way around your body and then back again.

CHAPTER 5

CARRYING AND LAUNCHING THE KAYAK

THE ADVICE WE OFFER IN THIS CHAPTER is really about avoiding injury. With today's lighter weight construction materials, better loading and roof rack systems, and even wheeled carts, getting your kayak to the water requires brains, not brawn.

Kayaks are most easily carried with a person at either end. An 80-pound (36 kg) tandem kayak is definitely a two-person lift. Take hold of a carrying toggle, or grab loop, at bow and stern. Remember to bend your legs, not your back, when you lift. Whenever a fully loaded single must be lifted, cup one hand under the end of the kayak so the toggle does not bear all the weight. A loaded tandem will require the assistance of several people on both ends and either side.

OPPOSITE When you are paddling in a coastal environment, where a prairie-size sky meets a distant horizon, the pink evening light becomes the color of everything.

RIGHT Even a child can carry an unloaded kayak using a two-person carry.

Solo Lift

You don't have to be particularly strong to lift a kayak solo. The trick is in getting it to your shoulder without hurting your back. Although the photos break the demonstration into five steps, the action is one fluid motion from knees to shoulder. A well-balanced kayak can be carried reasonably comfortably for a fair distance if you have some padding on your shoulder. Make sure you bend your legs and not your back when picking up the kayak.

1 Bend your knees, keeping your back straight. Grasp the inside edge of the cockpit rim. Establish the balance point of the kayak and then slide it up to your thighs.

2 Bend your knees, allowing the weight of the kayak to counter-balance you.

3 Use the momentum of straightening up to roll the kayak up to your shoulder. Simultaneously, your outside arm curls up, drawing the far edge of the cockpit rim to your shoulder.

4 Keeping your back straight throughout, turn your body to face the bow while tucking your supporting shoulder inside the cockpit.

5 Straighten your legs and use your opposite hand to steady the kayak. If you are walking some distance, place a folded towel or some kind of padding on your shoulder.

Kayak Cart

The easiest way to get the kayak to the water, if it is loaded and the terrain allows it, is a kayak cart. Rest the kayak's stern on the cart. Pack your gear in the kayak. Lift the bow and you are away. If the path is bumpy, strap the kayak to the cart so it doesn't fall off. If convenient, and you have the storage space, the cart folds up and can be packed into the kayak.

RIGHT The kayak cart is a simple device that can make getting even a fully loaded kayak to and from the water a cinch.

BELOW A tandem kayak is a nature discovery vehicle for a family on the water.

Car-topping

A safe and reliable roof rack and tie-down system is to your kayak what a seatbelt system is to passengers in a vehicle. But the kayak is on the outside of the car and is subject to enormous wind pressures both from the speed of travel and passing trucks. It doesn't take much imagination to envision disaster. Factory-installed roof racks on vehicles are not nearly as substantial as a solid set of racks specifically designed to carry outdoor gear. There is a wide range of adaptations for different vehicles and different kinds of equipment. A kayak cradle will hold a touring kayak in place safely and securely with the correct tie-down procedure.

We use 1-inch (2.5 cm) webbing straps with cam buckles because they are fast and reliable. Just make sure the straps lie flat and the rubber flap is between the kayak hull and the metal buckle. And watch when you toss the straps off that the buckle doesn't clunk down on the car roof!

Some 3/8-inch (1 cm) rope works well if you learn the tie-down system shown here. A few simple knots will help you tie down kayaks on trailers and roof racks. Tie the bow down to the vehicle's tow hooks or bumper, or try the method we have shown here of creating attachment points to the vehicle's frame between the hood and the fender.

If there are two or more of you, it is simplest and safest to lift a kayak up onto the roof racks with a partner. But since one of the great benefits of the touring kayak is enjoying the quiet pleasure of one's own company, it makes sense to learn the art of car-topping your kayak solo.

1 Place protective material under the stern to care for the kayak, and behind the bow rack to avoid scratching the vehicle roof. A piece of thin non-skid foam works very well for this, although you can use a folded towel.

2 Lift the bow and place it in the crook of the kayak cradle, making sure it will not slip. There are roof-rack extension bars available just for this job.

3 Lift the stern and slide the kayak forward.

4 Place the stern in the cradle, making sure that the crossbars on the roof rack system line up with a suitable place for your straps or tie-down ropes to cross over the kayak.

Tying the Kayak onto the Roof Rack

2 We attach two loops of rope to the vehicle frame at a place between the fender panel and the hood. Close the hood, leaving the loops on the outside as tie-down points for the bow of your kayak. Use the traveler's hitch (see Chapter 14) to secure the lines from the kayaks to these loops.

1 We prefer to use webbing straps for tie-downs. They are quick and secure. Once you have tied the kayaks on, wrap the loose webbing end in a series of neat loops around the crossbar. Using a couple of half hitches, secure the tail end of the webbing. Use cockpit covers to keep out the rain and other debris.

3 You can't afford to skimp on safety when it comes to car-top transport. It is a good rule to check, each time you stop en route to your paddling destination, to be sure that nothing has loosened up on the roof racks or in any knots or strapping.

Parallel Launching From Shore

This launch is useful in calm and or protected waters. More than once we have watched novice paddlers tip over before they even get in the kayak. This can be a good chuckle for all if the would-be paddler is dressed for a swim, the water is warm and no one gets hurt, but it is not the way most kayakers want to start out. You will discover that it is not the kayak that is tippy, just like a bicycle isn't tippy once you learn to ride it. It takes technique to be in balance.

If you are next to shore and the water is calm, the easiest approach is to swing the boat parallel to shore. By using the paddle as an outrigger, you can stabilize the kayak and slip in quite easily. Place the paddle across the back deck behind the cockpit so that it lies perpendicular to the kayak. The blade acting as the outrigger needs to be lying with the power face upward. This method works well when you do not have to step down. The paddle blade can rest on the bottom, on shore, or a low dock. (Keep your weight over the supported side of the kayak, getting in and out from this side only.) Hold the paddle shaft and the back of the cockpit rim together with one hand. Place the other hand on the shaft close to the kayak. (A paddle shaft can break if there is a great deal of weight placed in the middle of the bridge you have created with the paddle.) You can now sit temporarily on the back of the kayak. Slide one leg, then the other, into the cockpit. Then slide down into the seat. The key is to keep your weight over the supported side of the kayak.

1 **PARALLEL LAUNCHING FROM SHORE** Place the paddle perpendicular to the kayak and across the back deck behind the cockpit. The supporting blade is lying with the power face up.

2 Clamp the paddle shaft and coaming together with one hand (left hand in this photo).

Dock Launch

Getting in and out of your kayak from a dock can be a bit more challenging, especially if you have to step down a distance. The trick is to keep your weight on the supporting structure while at the same time keeping your weight centered over the kayak so it doesn't go shooting out from underneath you. At first, it is wise to get your sprayskirt secure while you still have the dock close at hand. Then pick your paddle up and you are ready to go.

1 **DOCK LAUNCH** Slip your feet into the cockpit, centering your weight over the kayak.

3 Depending on the size of your cockpit and the length of your legs, you can sit on the back deck temporarily while you get your legs into the cockpit.

4 Your other hand (right hand in photo) is placed on the paddle shaft close to the cockpit. Avoid placing a lot of weight in the center of the paddle shaft bridge. Slide into the kayak until you are seated comfortably all the while keeping pressure on the supporting paddle.

5 Bring the paddle forward and attach your sprayskirt. You are ready to go.

2 Turn your body so that it faces the supporting structure.

3 Lower yourself straight down into the cockpit. Depending on the length of your legs and the cockpit opening size, you may have to sit on the back deck temporarily before slipping inside the cockpit.

4 Slide down into the cockpit, maintaining your grip on the dock so you don't float away leaving your paddle behind! At this point, you have to use both hands to get the sprayskirt on. But the dock is there for support if you need it.

Launching Into Waves or Surf

This launch works well anytime there are waves breaking on shore. (A sideways launch will result in a cockpit full of water!) Place your kayak facing straight out to sea. If there are large waves washing in, you will have to watch them and decide how high up the beach you need to place the kayak so that you have time to get into the kayak and fasten the sprayskirt. Use your paddle on one side of the kayak, and your hand on the other side to work your way to the water. Once the kayak is floating, use strong forward strokes to move away from shore (and beyond the surf if this is the case).

If a wave is going to break over you, keep your kayak perpendicular to the waves as you break through them. Lean forward with your chest close to the deck. Just before you hit the wave, plant a powerful forward stroke. Drop your top hand so that you are holding your paddle parallel to the kayak just as the wave breaks over you. You don't want the wave to catch the flat face of your paddle, nor do you want to take the full force of a breaking wave on your torso. Be sure you are well out past the breaking point of the waves before you stop to look around.

OPPOSITE Inside the line of steep dumping surf, the smoother waves are a playground for skilled paddlers.

1 Practice surf launchings on an easy sloping beach. Many paddlers find this type of launch comforting because you can start out on a firm surface. Get the skirt attached as quickly as possible. Grab your paddle and begin working your way to the water.

2 Using a paddle blade on one side and a hand on the other, lift and shove the kayak down the beach. Watch the wave patterns and time your entry with the break between wave sets.

3 Once your kayak is floating, keep it perpendicular to shore. In big waves, this is critical; otherwise you will broach and find yourself washed up sideways to the shore.

4 Commit yourself and paddle strongly forward out beyond the breaking waves.

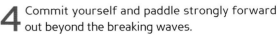

CHAPTER 6

THE FUNDAMENTALS OF PADDLING

A S PADDLERS, IT IS IMPORTANT TO UNDERSTAND that we, as a part of all of Nature, are subject to certain rules that dictate movement. It is also helpful to know that whether you are an expert or novice paddler, your body, paddle, kayak and the water all dance to these predictable rules. Understanding and applying this knowledge to your kayaking technique is important to becoming a smooth, efficient paddler.

Paddling Principles and Newton's Laws of Motion

Consider Isaac Newton's three Laws of Motion. First, a body will remain at rest or in constant motion until an outside force acts upon it. Second, the greater the force on a body, the greater its acceleration will be. Third, for every action there is an equal and opposite reaction. In kayaking, every stroke is an example of Newton's Laws at work. According to the third law, the action is the energy applied on the paddle blade by the paddler. The reaction is the response of the water molecules in the opposite direction to the energy applied. For practical purposes, we'll say the reaction is the response of the kayak, generally in the opposite direction. It is important to keep in mind that these laws are also at work when the external force is created by a wind or waves pushing against the hull of your kayak.

Early morning mist in Ontario's Ivanhoe Lake Provincial Park.

Physical Resistances That Affect the Kayak

As your kayak moves through the water there are three forms of resistance that act upon it. They are frontal, surface and eddy resistance. Frontal and eddy resistance create very different pressures on the kayak. By understanding and working with these forces, paddlers can execute strokes in the most effective and energy-saving manner.

Surface resistance is simply the friction of the water molecules acting on the hull of the kayak. Frontal resistance acts upon the leading end of the kayak, that is, whichever end is pushing through the water and wind. It exerts the greatest pressure on the kayak. If the kayak is going forward, the leading end, or frontal-resistance end, is the bow. If the kayak is going backward, it is the stern. As the kayak pushes through the water, the water presses in on each side of the kayak, providing a stabilizing effect up to its widest point (generally at the pivot point). Strokes executed at the leading end of the kayak are power strokes. As the kayak moves through space, it displaces water and air. Beyond the kayak's widest point, a vacuum is left to be filled by an unstable swirl of air and water. This is called the eddy-resistance end, or following end, of the kayak. Since there is little water pressure being exerted on this end of the kayak, turning and correction strokes have the most effect here.

If you are having trouble imagining this, let's make the kayak the stationary object and have the water flow around it. Think of your kayak secured to a marker buoy that is set in a river channel with a steady current flowing in it. Your kayak is tied at the bow. It will align itself with the current and, because it is tied at the bow, the bow is facing upstream. The water now hitting the bow of the kayak is acting in the same way that it does when you are paddling your kayak forward. The bow is the frontal-resistance end. As the water sweeps along the hull, it passes the widest point. When it does, a vacuum is created on either side of the hull. This vacuum must be filled with water that is drawn from the current. It actually swirls back upstream running contrary to the main current. The kayak has in effect created an eddy. Strokes placed in this eddy-resistance end of the kayak have the most effect on steering or turning. Understanding this bit of physics also explains why a rudder or a skeg is placed in the aft end of the kayak.

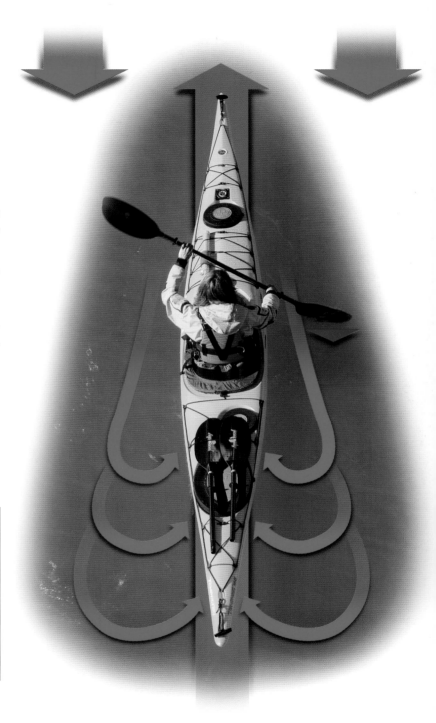

How to View the Illustrations

Force of the paddle against the water

Path traveled by the kayak

Force of the water against the kayak or paddle

The Pivot Point and a Well-Trimmed Kayak

The pivot point is a specific point on the bottom of the kayak where the total weight of the kayak is in balance. Since the pivot point is the point at which your kayak sinks most deeply in the water, it is the place where the kayak is initially most stable. It is also the point that most resists spinning or turning. It makes sense that in order to turn your kayak, the paddle blade should be placed as far from the pivot point as possible.

A well-trimmed kayak is balanced from side to side and from bow to stern. When the kayak is at rest in the water it is neither listing to one side nor the other, nor is it heavier at the bow or stern. When you pack your kayak, it is important to keep the kayak balanced. If it is bow-heavy, the kayak will be harder to paddle in a straight line. The weight will anchor the bow inviting the stern forward. This is especially noticeable in a following sea when you are traveling with the waves. A kayak that is stern heavy is sluggish. A kayak that lists to one side is hard on your spine and makes it awkward to paddle properly.

pivot point

OPPOSITE **Melting ice from the glacier on Sermitsiaq in Greenland cascades down the cliffs where the little black guillemots nest.**

The Paddle As Anchor

You don't have to aspire to be an Olympic sprinter or a marathon kayaker, but efficient paddling techniques that have evolved from the study of these athletes can benefit us all. Efficient paddling technique means not wasting your energy. Whether you are bucking a headwind or a tidal current, or you have a long day's travel ahead of you, knowing how to best use the energy you have is a wonderful thing.

When you plant the paddle blade, you want most of the energy to be transferred to the kayak. Theoretically, that means that the kayak moves past or around a stationary blade. A common mistake is to pull on the stroke before the blade is fully submerged. The energy you impart to the paddle is wasted in a lot of splashing and the stroke doesn't end up propelling you very far.

To understand this concept, think of planting your paddle in something thick and heavy like wet sand. You are pulling yourself in the kayak past the paddle. Although water is not wet sand and there is a bit of slippage, it really helps to concentrate on this concept.

Four Phases of a Stroke

Every stroke can be thought of in four phases, the wind-up, the catch, the propulsion, and the exit/recovery. However, as in walking, the movement is actually one continuous fluid motion repeated again and again. In kayaking, with two blade faces working on either side of the kayak, the catch and propulsion of one blade is simultaneously the recovery of the other.

THE WIND-UP Sit up straight in your seat, maintaining good posture. Hold your paddle with a relaxed grip throughout. Rotate your upper body, your torso, allowing your blade to be planted next to your toes. Plant your blade fully in the water. With your body in this wind-up position, you are ready for the propulsion phase of the stroke.

THE CATCH With your body in this wind-up position, plant your blade fully in the water. Try this exercise. Lock your arms and, without bending at the elbows, plant the blade and paddle forward. Although it may seem a little awkward, you can clearly feel that a lot of power comes from upper body rotation rather than the arm muscles. A common mistake is allowing your arms to do a lot of pushing and pulling. This is not efficient. The arm's range of motion is quite small compared to that of your torso.

THE WIND-UP

THE CATCH

Good posture means sitting upright, and it is just plain good for us whether we are sitting in a chair or paddling a kayak.

In any sport, posture plays an important role because it keeps us balanced and allows us to move with fluid, natural agility. When you have good posture in your kayak, you will find it much easier to rotate your upper body independently of your lower body, your strokes will be more powerful, and you will maintain control over your kayak's edging much more easily. When you have good posture, it is easier to have a relaxed stance. Although this upright sitting may actually be uncomfortable for some, we encourage you to work on it. Not only is it beneficial for kayaking, but it is surprisingly good for your overall health and you will be much happier getting out of bed in the morning when you are 88!

PROPULSION Once your blade is fully submerged, you pull on the paddle and unwind your upper body at the same time propelling your kayak through the water. Your real power for any stroke comes from the unwinding of your torso and the use of your stomach and side muscles.

THE EXIT/RECOVERY
The exit is the point at which the stroke ends and the blade gets removed from the water. Once the blade is out of the water, the recovery is the phase in which the blade is returning to the catch position.

PROPULSION

THE EXIT/RECOVERY

CHAPTER 7

GETTING CENTERED

F YOU ARE NOT RELAXED IN MIND AND BODY, it is hard to concentrate on learning anything, especially a sport such as kayaking. If you do not feel a natural sense of balance, you will constantly focus on capsizing. Instead of focusing on a tippy kayak, think of balance as something that happens between your body and gravity. These initial exercises such as Rock the Boat will help you loosen up and trust your balance. Being rigid and hesitant prevents you from moving smoothly and enjoying your kayak to the fullest.

J-Leaning Your Body and Edging the Kayak

No matter what kind of paddling you will be doing, you need to be comfortable with balancing your kayak on edge.

When we wish to put the kayak on its edge, or tilt the kayak for a turn, or "raise the side of opposition," as in a sideslip or an abeam, we refer to it as edging the kayak. In order to put the kayak on edge, you need to be loose in the hips, allowing your lower body to act independently of your upper body. This J-lean body position involves keeping your weight centered over the kayak.

To edge the kayak to the left, several things happen all at once. You will lift up with your right knee and thigh and your legs will hold a steady tilt on your kayak. It takes practice to keep the kayak steady and still. The left side of your body will be stretched and the right side of your body will be kinked. Your rib cage shifts to the left and your stomach and side muscles will be working to keep your body in an upright position.

Vice versa, to edge the kayak to the right, you will lift up with your left knee and thigh and the right side of your body is stretched and the left side curved into the J. Your upper body remains upright over your balance point with your legs holding the kayak steady.

This boat control does require practice, but it is a fundamental building block for good kayaking technique. As you become comfortable with both sides, you can work on transferring your weight back and forth quickly from edge to edge. This is an exercise we call "Rock the Boat." A more advanced challenge, but nevertheless an excellent exercise, is to practice holding an edge while paddling forward. (See Forward Stroke in Chapter 8, Strokes and Maneuvers).

1 With the correct upright posture and snug-fitting seat, you will benefit most from each stroke you take because the energy from your body will be transferred to the kayak most efficiently. You should have good contact with the boat at your feet, knees, thighs and hips. The balls of your feet should be resting on the foot braces and your knees should be braced under the deck.

2 "Rock the Boat" is an exercise that emphasizes the necessary independence between your upper and lower body. It will assure you that it is not the kayak that is tippy, but merely your lack of balance that makes it so. With your hips loose, lift up alternately with first one knee then the other to rock the kayak from edge to edge while keeping your upper body upright. Rock the kayak quickly then slowly, and then hold the edge for a few moments on each side.

3 Holding your paddle overhead, use one knee then the other to pull the kayak up into the edge position. This means of stretching one side of your body while bending the other side of your body to rock the boat develops balance, and it is essential for good kayaking technique. If you do this in a "snappy" fashion, you have the makings of an effective "hip snap." It is this knee lift and hip snap that you will use while bracing and, later, rolling the kayak.

OPPOSITE When you are paddling over a shallow sandy bottom on a sunny day, as here near Pukaskwa, your shadow becomes your companion.

Bracing Strokes

In any sport, people lose their balance from time to time, and kayaking is no exception. The important thing is not to worry about losing it but rather concentrate on being able to recover from it. In fact, when you have a really bombproof brace, you can practically turn the kayak over and still recover without even getting your hair wet!

The low brace and the high brace are the two recovery strokes we are demonstrating here. Both of these strokes involve reaching out to the side of the kayak (the side that you are falling toward), slapping the water with the paddle blade while lifting up with your lower knee, and doing a hip snap. There are differences between the two that we will discuss, but the most important thing to understand is that the paddle blade only provides momentary support. Your body is actually responsible for righting the kayak. As your kayak tips, it is the action of pulling up with the knee (on the side you are capsizing toward) and your loose hips that really recover you before a capsize.

The action of the head is a very important part of the success or failure to recover. The only way to pull up with this lower knee is to drop your head

TIP DROP YOUR HEAD

Dropping your head in the direction of the capsize is essential for a righting stroke to be effective. Lifting your head actually results in lifting the high knee (the wrong knee) and tipping you in even faster. While practicing your righting strokes, keep your eyes on the paddle blade as it slaps the water. This action tends to draw your head toward the water where it needs to be.

in the direction you are tipping. But throwing your head toward the water does not feel like it is going to help matters at all. The natural tendency is to lift your head up. Unfortunately this is exactly what prevents you from lifting the correct knee (the low knee) and more often than not results in a capsize. Dropping your head in the direction you are falling lowers your center of gravity, allowing your lower knee to pull up and your hips to swing freely to roll the kayak back upright.

The sculling high brace is shown as an advanced maneuver to demonstrate just how far you can take a brace before a roll or other capsize recovery will be necessary.

1 Here's a way to develop good reflexes for your bracing strokes. One partner stands in the water at the stern of the kayak while the other sits in the kayak with the paddle resting at 90 degrees to the deck.

2 The person in the water gives the kayak a sudden hearty twist to one side or the other, edging the kayak enough to encourage the paddler to respond with low braces and high braces.

3 Since the paddler does not know when or which way the kayak will tip, she has to respond without warning. Developing an instinctive bracing reaction in this exercise helps you respond faster in normal paddling conditions.

The Low Brace

The low brace is the ideal recovery technique because it involves keeping your paddle quite low, which helps keep your shoulder safe. Sitting upright, set up the low brace by laying the paddle at 90 degrees to the deck of the kayak. Place your hands on the shaft with your forearms in a vertical push-up position. Your knuckles face down. Start by practicing the upper body action only. Keep the kayak flat on the water while reaching out to slap the water. Your shaft angle remains horizontal and the shaft stays close to your body. As you slap the surface, drop your head toward the water. Once you get comfortable with this, then you can edge the kayak in the direction you are bracing, and incorporate the lower body action of the knee lift and hip snap. Tip the kayak and reach the paddle out toward the water. Maintain a low shaft angle 90 degrees to the deck of the kayak. Your hands remain low; one is at your stomach and the other over the water. Simultaneously drop your head sideways toward the water and smack the water with the back face of the paddle blade. Lift up with your low knee. (If you are tipping to the right, it is your right knee that is lifting.) After slapping the water, pull your paddle slightly forward and inward continuing to keep your head low and your lower knee lifting. Roll your knuckles upward to slice the blade from the water.

Practice this action on alternating sides to ensure your paddle blade hits the water flat. This is especially important to practice with a feathered paddle. You will need to rotate your shaft to slap the surface with a flat blade.

1 Place the paddle at 90 degrees to the deck of your kayak. Place your hands on the paddle shaft knuckles down, forearms vertical in a push-up position. Edge the kayak to one side.

2 With one hand at your stomach, and one hand over the water, slap, or push down, on the water with the paddle's back face, keeping the blade flat to the water. While you are doing this, drop your head toward the water. It helps to keep your eyes on the paddle blade.

3 Simultaneously while slapping the water, lift up with your lower knee (the one on the paddle action side of the kayak). Pull your paddle slightly forward and inward. Keep your head low. (Think of putting your ear to your shoulder.) Remember you are only weighting the paddle momentarily.

4 Roll your knuckles upward so the blade is on a slight climbing angle to clear the surface. By this time, your recovery action is happening mostly with your knee lift and with very little weight on the blade. Keep your head low toward the water so that the lower knee can continue lifting the kayak upright.

The High Brace

The high brace is the most powerful recovery technique. Since it is essentially the final phase of the roll, a paddler with a good high brace can recover even when his or her kayak is almost fully upside-down. As well, it seems that the high brace position feels the most natural. These two factors result in it being relied upon often more than it should be. The risk with the high brace is the frequency with which shoulder injuries occur. Despite the name high brace, it is very important to adopt a low stance with the arms. The paddle needs to be lower than your shoulders and in front of your body.

The degree to which you perform the high brace depends, as it does with the low brace, on whether it is being used to correct a minor tip or a point-of-no-return capsize. Sitting upright, set up the high brace. The paddle shaft is 90 degrees to the deck of the kayak. Pick up the paddle with your knuckles facing up. Your forearms are almost vertical with your elbows down. Your arms are in a chin-up position on the paddle shaft. You can start this exercise by keeping your kayak flat and concentrating on the paddle action and the head drop. Add the edging of the kayak lower body action once you feel comfortable with what your upper body is going to do. Edge, or tip, your kayak. Reach out over the water, keeping the paddle shaft at 90 degrees to the kayak, and the shaft angle as low as possible. Keep the elbow on your top arm tucked into your body.

The more you paddle, the more you will find the powerful high brace coming to your rescue in the nick of time.

1 Hold the paddle, dropping your elbows down so that your arms are in a chin-up position. Your knuckles face up. Edge, or tip, the kayak. Slap the water with the power face of the blade. Keep your elbows tucked in close to the body.

2 Simultaneously drop your head and lift up with your lower knee. (Keep your head down until you are fully recovered. Either watch the paddle or keep your ear to your shoulder.) Pull your paddle slightly forward and inward, bracing only briefly.

3 Most of the recovery comes from your lower body action — the lifting of that lower knee while pressing the opposite buttock into the seat. The paddle blade clears the water on a slight climbing angle. Do this exercise back and forth on both sides while challenging yourself to edge more and more each time.

Sculling High Brace

Imagine yourself spreading peanut butter on bread — this is just about the action you are performing with your sculling blade. This maneuver shows you just how much steady and sustained support you can get from your paddle blade as long as it is in continuous motion on the surface of the water. In fact, you can exaggerate this action to the point of practically overturning the kayak without actually capsizing!

Start the sculling high brace in the ready position with the paddle resting at 90 degrees to the deck of the kayak. Pick up the paddle in the high brace "chin-up" arm position. Place the power face of the paddle on the surface and start a rhythmic sculling motion tracing an elongated figure eight. The key is to keep your paddle moving and your

blade on a climbing angle. This climbing angle means that the paddle's leading edge is higher than its trailing edge.

The paddle will rise to the surface instead of diving to the bottom. Keep even pressure on the blade and use torso rotation to move it through the water. When sculling, you have to cock your wrists back as you push the paddle forward and curl your wrists forward as you pull the paddle back.

Begin by gently edging the kayak. Feel the lift of your lower knee and the J-lean position of your body. As you edge the kayak more and more, maintain a strong, smooth movement with the paddle and continue tracing the figure eight. Aim to get the lower edge of the your cockpit wet. Eventually you can submerge most of your torso and get your head wet too!

CHAPTER 8

Strokes and Maneuvers

THIS IS THE PART YOU HAVE BEEN WAITING FOR. You are in the kayak, you feel relatively balanced and you are ready to go somewhere! It's time to learn strokes and maneuvers. Remember that strokes are performed with the paddle, while maneuvers are what happen to the kayak. Repeated strokes or combinations of different strokes result in kayak maneuvers. In this chapter, we cover sweep strokes to spin or turn the kayak, draw strokes to move the kayak sidesways, and propulsion strokes to move you in a straight line. We look at how to stop a kayak, U-turn a kayak while on the move, and how to sideslip to move the kayak sideways while maintaining forward momentum. Finally, we take a peek at the exciting environment of moving water, both on rivers and in the surf.

OPPOSITE You need never go farther than a place like this to find complete satis-faction paddling your kayak. Some seek a thrill from the sport but most people merely wish to carve a silent path of their own making on the water.

RIGHT Negotiating the turbulent seas of October at the mouth of Lake Superior's Michipicoten River.

Spins

The forward and reverse sweep strokes are used to spin the kayak or correct its course. Begin with the kayak flat on the water. The smooth arcing motion of a spinning kayak is a result of planting the blade as far from the centerpoint as possible and rotating your torso. The name "sweep stroke" is a bit misleading, as you should think of the kayak as moving around the stationary blade. When you are comfortable with the kayak flat, then edge the kayak and adjust the blade angle to provide more support. Watch the blade throughout the stroke to ensure torso rotation.

Let's look at why edging makes the spin so much more effective. The hull of a touring kayak has a fairly straight keel line to help it go straight ahead most easily. We can alter the hull shape of the kayak in the water (its footprint) if we put the kayak on edge. The more you edge your kayak, the more rockered the kayak's footprint and therefore the better it will spin. To help you maintain your balance and keep a steady edge while tilted and spinning, put a slight climbing angle on your sweep stroke to lend some bracing support. This is important knowledge, and once you understand it and adopt it, you will find turning the kayak much, much easier.

> TIP Be sure your rudder is up or your skeg is retracted so that it doesn't interfere with your learning. The rudder blade needs to be resting in its rudder rest so that your foot braces are in a fixed position.

1 FORWARD SWEEP Fully rotate your torso. Anchor the blade as close to the kayak's center-line as possible, and completely submerge it. Your hands and the shaft angle are both low. Edge the kayak away from the direction in which you are spinning.

2 Apply force to the power face by unwinding your upper body. Follow the blade's path with your eyes and keep your shoulders aligned with the paddle shaft. The kayak will smoothly spin away from the planted blade. With a low shaft angle, you can get the blade as far from the hull as possible.

3 To get the most power from your torso, push on the foot brace on the sweeping side of the kayak. (In this demonstration, the kayaker is pushing on the right foot brace while spinning to the left.)

4 Continue to fully rotate your upper body until the stern almost meets the paddle blade. Roll your knuckles and wrists forward, which feathers the blade smoothly from the water. (Do this before the blade gets pinned against the hull).

5 The recovery is one smooth motion in which the shaft angle is kept low and the blade is feathered back to the bow as your upper body rotates for the next stroke.

6 With your torso fully rotated, plant the blade at the bow and repeat, remembering to keep your eyes on the blade to ensure torso rotation.

Reverse Sweep

A reverse sweep (or back sweep) is a turning stroke that starts at the stern of the kayak and traces a wide arcing path to the bow. It uses the back face of the blade. It is a stroke that can be used to spin a kayak or help it change direction. In changing direction, the reverse sweep effectively stops the kayak.

1 **REVERSE SWEEP** Start by rotating your torso to face the side on which you will be sweeping. Both hands are over the water with knuckles down. Plant the blade near the stern as close to the centerline as possible.

2 Using the back face of your paddle, plant the blade with a slight climbing angle. Edge the kayak toward the side you are sweeping on and start unwinding your torso.

3 Continue applying pressure to the back face of the blade and keep the shaft angle low as you unwind your torso. Press your foot against the foot brace on the sweep side—the right foot if you are doing a back sweep on the right side.

4 Continue to maintain a low shaft angle through out the reverse sweep. Watch the submerged blade throughout the stroke to ensure torso rotation.

5 The blade angle can be adjusted by rolling your knuckles forward a bit to provide more support if needed.

6 Keep spinning the kayak around the blade until it nearly reaches the bow. Slip the blade out of the water near your feet by rolling your knuckles back.

Combination Forward and Reverse Sweeps

Performing a forward sweep on one side immediately followed by a reverse sweep on the other is a very effective way to spin a stationary kayak. In a solo kayak, work on perfecting a smooth transition from edge to edge as you transition between a forward sweep, back sweep, forward sweep.

Similarly, the quickest and most efficient way to reposition a tandem kayak to face in another direction is to spin it using forward and reverse sweeps. To perform this spin, the bow and stern paddlers work together in unison doing opposing sweeps. Remember, the further the blade is from the pivot point, the more effectively it turns the kayak. In the tandem situation, therefore, the bow and stern paddlers need only complete half a sweep — a 90-degree arc — from stern to hip (for the reverse sweep) and hip to bow (forward sweep).

1 **TANDEM SPIN** The bow paddler begins by rotating his torso to prepare for a forward sweep. The stern paddler rotates her torso to prepare for a reverse sweep.

2 The bow paddler plants the blade with a low shaft angle as far forward (as far from the pivot point) as possible. The stern paddler plants the blade in the same way, but toward the stern, as far from the pivot point as possible.

3 The kayak remains relatively flat as both paddlers begin to unwind their torsos. The kayak spins away from the planted blades at bow and stern.

4 When the blades are at a point opposite each paddler's hip, the recovery begins. The bow paddler rolls his knuckles forward to smoothly feather the blade from the water. The stern paddler rolls her knuckles back to also feather the blade from the water.

5 Both paddlers return their blades to the catch position, keeping a low shaft angle. The paddlers' torsos are winding up for the next stroke.

Abeams, or Moving Sideways

It is a very handy thing to be able to move sideways without turning your kayak, and to be able to do it from a stationary position. It allows you to come alongside another kayak to have a chat, share a snack or look at the map. It also enables you to pull up to a dock or the shore.

The first stroke we will look at is the draw stroke, or T-stroke. This stroke involves reaching out to the side of your kayak, planting your blade and pulling your hip to the blade. (Since efficient paddling technique means that our goal is to move the kayak, not the paddle, we are going to continue to insist that you are drawing the kayak to the paddle, not the paddle to the kayak.) Rotate your torso to face the direction in which you are traveling. Fully submerge the blade with the power face facing you. Your blade needs to remain opposite your pivot point in order to move directly sideways. If you find your bow being drawn toward the blade, then the blade is too far forward. If the blade is too far back, then you will be drawing the stern to the blade. Raise the side of opposition, in other words, if you are traveling left, lift up your left knee and thigh. We have used two colored buoys to give a sense of how the kayak is traveling across the water.

1 DRAW STROKE WITH IN-WATER RECOVERY
Rotate your torso to face the direction in which you are traveling. Fully submerge the blade away from the hull with the power face turned toward you. Your knuckles face back. Your top hand is near your forehead and the paddle shaft is relatively vertical.

2 To edge the kayak and avoid pushing all that unnecessary water, raise the side of opposition, lifting with your knee on the side you are traveling toward. Unwind your torso, drawing your hip to the blade.

3 Continue unwinding your torso until your blade is nearly at the hull. Turn your knuckles forward, which alters the pitch of the underwater blade so that it is perpendicular to the hull and ready for the underwater recovery.

4 Slice the blade back out to the catch position fully underwater. Keep the blade opposite the kayak's pivot point to prevent the kayak from turning toward the bow or stern.

Sculling Draw

The action of the sculling draw is much like that of the sculling brace in the previous chapter, Getting Centered, only the paddle shaft is now held in a more vertical position. Sculling with a raised side of opposition moves your kayak more gracefully than does the draw stroke with in-water recovery. Another way to understand the sculling action is to extend your arm out toward the water with your palm flat and facing down. Pretend you are treading water by repeatedly tracing the outline of a figure eight with your hand above the surface. Now drop your arm down so your fingers point to the water. This is the position your paddle will be in. The entire stroke is simply propulsion. There is no catch and recovery phase. Think of your torso, arms and paddle as one unit moving smoothly together along a short path forward and backward a foot or two out to the side of your kayak. If the figure eight has balanced pressure during both loops and is performed evenly on either side of the kayak's pivot point, the kayak will move straight sideways.

A great drill is to place your kayak perpendicular to a dock. Your bow should be a few inches away from the edge of it. Now see if you can use a sculling draw to travel sideways while maintaining both the perpendicular relation to the dock (your bow does not start getting ahead of your stern) and the kayak's distance from the dock. The closer you can travel without touching, and the faster you can move, the more fun this game becomes.

1 SCULLING DRAW Fully rotate your body to face the direction in which you are traveling. Your top hand is near your forehead. Your paddle shaft is fairly vertical. Your other arm is tucked in, elbow down. Begin by cocking your knuckles and wrists on both hands back to open the power face toward the bow. Rotate your torso toward the bow for the first part of the sculling action.

2 Then roll your knuckles and wrists forward, which will change the pitch of your underwater blade, angling it toward the stern. Rotate your torso as you slice the blade back toward the stern. Maintain smooth pressure on the blade as the sculling action carves out a figure eight. Maintain the raised side of opposition throughout.

3 When you hold a steady J-lean (which does require some balance practice), the edged kayak will move smoothly and gracefully sideways. Keep the paddle blade moving along a short path forward and backward a foot or two out to the side of your kayak.

Power or Propulsion Strokes

Up to this point, we have demonstrated two of the three categories of strokes: righting strokes and corrective strokes. The third category is the power or propulsion strokes, the ones that propel you in a straight line, whether forward or backward.

Moving Forward

Since traveling forward is what you do most of the time in a touring kayak, we are going to touch on some of the basics covered in Chapter 6 and spend a few pages looking at this single most important stroke from different perspectives. We hope this will help you become a more efficient forward paddler, enabling you to paddle longer more comfortably and with more power.

Begin learning (or improving) your forward stroke by lifting your rudder or skeg, if you have one. Remember the feeling of removing the training wheels on your bicycle? Skegs and rudders have their place, but if you make a habit of paddling without their help, you will find your technique improves immeasurably.

In the next series of images, we have demonstrated both the forward stroke with a lower shaft angle commonly used for touring and, on page 80, the more aggressive power forward, which uses a more vertical paddle shaft angle. Because the power forward exaggerates all the qualities of the most efficient forward stroke, we feel it is excellent exercise to work on this whenever you can. There are times such as in a rescue situation where sprinting forward can mean all the difference!

The forward stroke starts with sitting up straight. Your legs are in the diamond position with your feet on the foot braces. Rotate your torso all the way from the base of your spine. You are not just moving your shoulders. This full rotation is the motion that gives your forward stroke its power. The muscles of your abdomen, torso and back are driving the stroke while your arm muscles are supplementary, for holding and lifting the paddle. Just practice this full rotating motion from left to right before you even begin paddling. While you are doing this, try to keep the kayak flat on the water. (Shifting the hips back and forth causes the kayak to rock from side to side and is a common problem while kayaking.) Let's start with a stroke on your right side.

THE WIND-UP AND THE CATCH Wind up your torso with your right shoulder forward. (The wind-up also enables you to reach further forward to your toes for the catch.) Lift your left elbow to align it with your shoulder and your hand. Your elbows have a relaxed bend in them and are not rigid. You are going to plant and fully submerge the paddle blade into the water beside your right foot. The paddle shaft is relatively vertical (depending on how aggressive your forward stroke is going to be), and the blade is perpendicular to the hull.

Now for the **PROPULSION** phase, where you unwind your torso. Since most of the forward stroke's power happens at the beginning, it is to your benefit to make the most of it. Simultaneously unwind your torso and push your right foot into the foot brace. All the power in your upper body is being transferred to the paddle to move you forward. Your elbows will remain slightly bent and relaxed, not rigid. The stroke ends when your right hand reaches your hip.

THE EXIT If you hold the blade in the water past your hip, you will be lifting water, which is inefficient. Unlike canoeing, where there is a rest in each recovery stroke, the double-bladed kayak paddle allows for only a brief respite at this point between when the blade on the right exits the water and the left blade is planted in the catch.

Now try linking a few strokes together. Don't worry about speed; it will increase as your stroke grows naturally more graceful and fluid. It is more important to develop a comfortable cadence, a rhythm that you can maintain. Soon you will be gliding effortlessly through the water mile after mile.

Tandem kayaks are ideal for traveling with children or for two paddlers of different strength and ability who wish to paddle together. The stern paddler steers while both paddlers provide propulsion; if one person wishes to rest, the other can carry on paddling.

1 FORWARD STROKE: THE WIND-UP Rotate your torso to allow the blade to be planted as far forward as possible (in this case, on the right side). Lift your elbow in line with your shoulder and forearm.

2 THE CATCH Plant the blade, making sure it is fully submerged and the power face is perpendicular to the hull. (This shaft angle can be increased to vertical for the power forward stroke.)

3 PROPULSION Unwind your torso. The main thrust comes from the use of the abdomen, side and back muscles. Press your foot (the right one in this case) against the foot brace. Keep the right shoulder, the bent elbow and the wrist aligned.

4 **THE EXIT** The propulsion phase ends when your lower hand reaches your hip. Slice the blade up and out of the water.

5 **THE RECOVERY** When the paddle blade exits the water at your hip, this brief rest between strokes is also the wind-up for the catch on your other side.

In our days spent paddling the Sea of Cortez off Espirito Santo Island, Baja, Mexico, we kept our binoculars at the ready to watch the wildlife. We saw gray whales, sea lions and over a hundred different species of birds including brown pelicans and blue-footed boobies.

Power Forward

This is the stroke to use when you need speed. This can be a prolonged sprint such as when the wind is picking up and you need to complete your crossing of open water, or you need a burst of speed when you are launching your kayak through surf, catching waves or assisting in a rescue situation. Core components that make the power forward more powerful than the forward stroke are more torso rotation at the catch, a fully submerged blade planted further forward near the toes, and a strong unwinding of the body while maintaining a vertical paddle shaft throughout the stroke.

ABOVE The power forward emphasizes more torso rotation and a higher shaft angle, enabling you to plant the blade further forward and unwind with a more aggressive action. The added power at the catch provides a more powerful propulsion phase. The propulsion phase is shorter and quicker than in a touring forward stroke.

OPPOSITE A good exercise for boat control and balance is to practice paddling straight ahead while maintaining a J-lean and edging your kayak. Paddle for a distance holding the kayak on edge on one side and then switch to the other side.

Edge Control While Paddling Forward

Once you are comfortable with your forward stroke, practice paddling forward in a straight line while holding your kayak steady and on edge. Switch from one edge to the other every dozen strokes or so. We referred to this edge-control exercise in Chapter 7, Getting Centered. Now try something else. Start out paddling forward. In this exercise, you will allow the kayak to turn away from the direction in which you are edging (tilting) your kayak. The more you edge your kayak, the more aggressively your kayak will turn.

Learn to steer your kayak with edging — it is a great skill to master, and with it you can make small corrections while forward paddling without losing any speed. It will help you deal with wind, wave action and current that makes staying on track more difficult.

TIPS PROBLEM SOLVING

PROBLEM Your kayak rocks from side to side.
SOLUTION Your hips are shifting back and forth as you paddle. Rotate your torso, sit flat and push with your feet — the left foot during the left paddle stroke, and right foot for the right stroke.

PROBLEM Your kayak bounces up and down.
SOLUTION Keep your upper body quiet and straight. Just rotate it. Try to prevent yourself from leaning forward and backward.

PROBLEM You are splashing at the beginning of each stroke.
SOLUTION Make sure the blade is fully planted before you unwind and take that stroke. Splashing is a lot of wasted energy.

PROBLEM Tendonitis in your wrist or forearm.
SOLUTION This is caused by the repetitive bending of the wrist. Keep the shoulder, elbow, forearm and wrist aligned as you unwind taking the stroke. The wrist should not bend.

PROBLEM Forearm fatigue.
SOLUTION Relax your top hand's grip by opening your fingers on the shaft during each stroke. This also ensures that you are not bending your wrist. (If you are, you will drop the paddle.)

PROBLEM Your arms get really tired.
SOLUTION Paddle using the muscles of your torso, not those smaller arm muscles. Maintain a fixed arm position without bending and straightening the arm.

Back Stroke

Although it seems as if the back stroke should be easy because it is just the opposite of the forward stroke, it turns out that it is a bit trickier. Think of climbing down a rock face that was easy to climb up; now, when you are descending, it isn't as easy to see your feet or where they are going next! It simply isn't as instinctive a feeling as moving forward. But the back stroke plays a valuable role and is important to learn. A few quick successive back strokes are what we use to stop. If you are in a rescue situation, back paddling effectively can be critical. The back stroke is used frequently while paddling in surf or current.

The back stroke uses the back face of the blade so there is no need to change your grip or rotate the paddle. Torso rotation in the back stroke serves two important functions; it provides the power but it also allows you to look behind you to watch where you are going.

The stroke starts just behind your hip and ends at your toes. Wind up your torso so that your upper body is facing the side that you are taking the stroke on. Plant the paddle completely submerging the blade. When the blade reaches your toes, slice it up and out of the water. You are now in the wind-up position, ready for the catch on the opposite side. To provide more support, a lower shaft angle can be adopted while back paddling in surf or current.

Be sure to look over your shoulder on every other stroke so you can watch where you are going and avoid obstacles.

1 **BACK STROKE** Rotate your torso and look over your shoulder in the direction in which you are headed.

2 Plant the blade in the water slightly behind your hip. Remember to keep within the Paddler's Box.

3 Apply pressure on the back face of the blade while rotating your torso forward. Although you do feel your lower hand pushing forward, think of the real power as coming from your unwinding torso so you don't get into "arm paddling" mode.

4 The blade exits the water by your feet. The kayak should be traveling in a straight line backward.

5 Rotate your torso through to the catch on the other side, with your head continuing to look forward. Look back over your shoulder on every other stroke.

Sideslipping Forward

With abeams, we can move a stationary kayak sideways with dynamic draw strokes. With sideslipping, we can take advantage of the kayak's forward speed and move it sideways while underway using a static stroke called a hanging draw. This maneuver is useful in that it allows you to avoid obstacles without having to turn, change direction or sacrifice speed. Let's say you are paddling along next to shore and all of a sudden you spy a rock dead ahead. Instead of putting on the brakes (it might be too late anyway), just sideslip around the obstacle without ever losing speed. Sideslipping is simple and easy to learn. Practice with soft, moveable targets such as these anchored red markers buoys and you will find yourself concentrating much more on the maneuver than worrying about colliding with something.

Our purpose in this exercise is to shift or sideslip the kayak sideways between the buoys without allowing the kayak to spin forward or backward. The sideslip maneuver requires forward momentum in order to create a force against the static blade position. Place the blade in the water just ahead of your hip and let the water act against it. (If the blade is put in too far forward, it will cause the bow to turn toward the blade. Just slide the blade back a little until you can feel the whole kayak being drawn sideways.) With this hanging draw, concentrate on the blade angle. It points in the direction in which you want to go. It doesn't matter if you sideslip forward or backward, this rule holds true. While sideslipping, it is important to raise your side of opposition to reduce the resistance against the hull as you move laterally across the water. If you need to continue moving sideways after the kayak has lost momentum with the sideslip, then you convert your stationary stroke into a sculling draw (see pages 74 to 75).

1 FORWARD SIDESLIP You need forward momentum before initiating the sideslip. To see what is happening in the sideslip, practice with a couple of markers spaced a kayak length apart, and you will develop finesse and accuracy with sideslipping.

2 On passing the first buoy, edge the kayak (raise the side of opposition) so that there is less water resistance against the hull. The blade is positioned in a stationary draw with the leading edge of the blade angled in the direction you are headed.

3 Continue holding the kayak on edge. Maintain the static draw position just forward of your hip and the kayak will sideslip laterally without spinning forward or backward.

4 The single most important thing to know about sideslips is that the leading edge of the blade angles in the direction in which you want to go, whether you are sideslipping forward or backward.

5 The paddler maintains a static position throughout. It is the kayak's forward momentum and the action of the water moving against the blade that draw the kayak sideways. To continue moving sideways after you have lost momentum, turn the static draw into a sculling draw.

Sideslipping Backward

Practice sideslipping backward. The purpose of this exercise is to get yourself thinking more about how the force of the water is acting upon your kayak and paddle to draw you sideways. The oncoming water makes no distinction between bow and stern. The stern has in effect become the bow and everything is exactly like sideslipping forward. You have to imagine you have eyes in the back of your head and that your stern is actually your bow. Then you just need to think about opening up the leading edge of the blade to the oncoming water and raising the side of opposition. The challenge is to control the placement of the blade; if too far forward or back, the kayak will spin.

1 BACKWARD SIDESLIP Just as with sideslipping forward, you need momentum before initiating the sideslip backward. Back paddle and then plant the blade near your hip. The leading edge of the blade points in the direction in which you want to sideslip.

2 Hold the kayak on edge with the side of opposition raised. This will make the sideways movement smoother and faster.

3 Keep your lower elbow tucked in and your top arm near your forehead. The shaft angle is high and the blade is kept in a static position near your hip. Adjust the blade's position near your hip if the kayak is turning. (If the kayak is turning toward the stern, move the blade slightly forward or vice versa.)

4 Continue holding the blade in a static position, allowing the moving water to act against the kayak and paddle to draw you sideways.

5 Once momentum as slowed, turn your static stroke into an abeam sculling the kayak sideways.

Stopping

A series of three or four quick alternating back strokes is an effective way to stop. If you are approaching an obstacle such as a rock (a floating buoy is forgiving for practice), and you wish to stop quickly, drop the blade in next to your hip and completely submerge it. You are going to absorb all that forward energy, so keep your wrists in line with your forearms to prevent wrist strain. Slice the blade out when it is only halfway through the stroke.

1 STOPPING Power forward until you are about 10 feet (3 m) from your target. Then plant a quick, short backstroke on one side.

2 Immediately rotate your torso and plant a quick, short backstroke on the other side.

3 You should be able to come to a full stop with three or four strokes. If your strokes are quick, crisp and short, your kayak should not waver much from side to side.

4 Practice with a buoy so that you become proficient at knowing exactly how close you can get before putting in the series of choppy backstrokes to brake in time.

U-Turns

A U-turn is a 180-degree change in direction while on the move. There are several ways to make U-turns in a kayak. When practicing, it is helpful to have a fixed point such as our anchored red marker around which to turn. Keep in mind three things while doing U-turns: you need speed, the kayak needs to be edging into the turn, and it needs to be angled in the direction of the turn.

The Low Brace U-Turn

The most basic and fundamental of all moving turns is the low brace turn. This is a maneuver that comes in handy in all kinds of situations. It combines the forward sweep and a reverse sweeping low brace ending on a power forward stroke on that same side. The turn supports the paddler as long as the paddler has speed. Edging the kayak is very important, but it is good to keep in mind that as the kayak reaches the end of its turn, it slows down and the amount of support you will get from your brace drops considerably, so you will have to adjust your balance accordingly. Apply less edging and start flattening the kayak out at the end of the turn. As with all maneuvers, our goal is to transition from one stroke smoothly into the next. This is what makes you a graceful paddler.

1 **LOW BRACE U-TURN** Get up some speed and initiate the turn with a forward sweep. If you are turning to the left, then your sweep will be on the right as in the photograph.

2 Rotate your upper body and edge the kayak into the turn. Your blade initiates a reverse sweeping low brace.

3 Your knuckles are turned down as you are in the push-up position of the low brace. The more speed you have, the more you can put your kayak on edge into the turn.

4 Your blade sweeps forward to a point directly out to the side from your hip. There should be a climbing angle on the blade so that it provides both support and turning power. Your kayak is turning around this low brace.

5 Keep bringing the blade forward as you unwind your torso until the shaft is in a vertical position with the blade planted near your toes in the catch position for the power forward.

6 Finish the U-turn on a strong power forward.

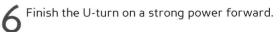

The High Brace U-Turn

This powerful, high-speed turn enables you to turn 180 degrees with surprising agility. The high brace turn uses an initial forward sweep and a high brace position for support. As with the low brace turn, the high brace turn requires speed to support the brace. Once the turn is made and the kayak slows down, reduce your edging to flatten it out and transition into a power forward.

1 **HIGH BRACE U-TURN** An anchored marker buoy is an excellent tool for practicing this important maneuver. Start with forward speed and initiate the turn with a forward sweep.

2 Edge the kayak into the turn.

3 Plant the blade with the power face angled toward the bow. This means cocking back the wrist on your lower hand.

4 The kayak turns around the planted blade. The climbing angle on the blade allows you to get steady support from it as your kayak continues to move forward.

5 To protect your shoulder, stay within the Paddler's Box and keep your lower arm tucked into your body.

6 Once the kayak has turned around the planted paddle and the turn is complete, the paddle is now in the catch position of the forward stroke.

Learning About Current

Paddling in a current can be intimidating, but once you know how it works and have mastered the necessary skills, you can have fun and feel more comfortable anywhere you encounter moving water. Current is found on rivers, in ocean tides and on big inland lakes. Wind compounds the effects of current. When there is current, there is a force moving the water. That force can be the earth's gravitational pull as in the flow of a river, or the moon's, which results in the ocean's tides. One of the best ways to find out how moving water behaves is to visit a river.

Start by simply watching the flowing water. Notice the relatively calm areas that form behind features that obstruct the main current. When the current is deflected around an obstruction, an eddy forms where the water curls in behind it. For this reason, eddies themselves can be calm, and they can have their own upstream current, which moves in the opposite direction of the main current. An eddy line forms where the eddy and the main current collide. As would be expected, eddy lines are a scramble. They don't know which way to flow, and it is easy to see why this not a desirable place to be. The stronger the main current, the stronger the eddy lines will be. Whirlpools are common along an eddy line.

Shown in the next two sequences is a suitable setting for practicing ferrying and getting in and out of eddies. This location has a warm water current with two well-defined eddies on either side, a deep run-out and easy upstream paddling to make repeated ferries, eddy turns and peel-outs. Novices will feel more comfort-

able committing to their J-leans and edging if the worst that can happen is a swim in a deep, calm pool. Beware of shallow, fast-moving current with obstructions, which can prove a dangerous situation for the inexperienced. Always consider the possibility of a capsize and what the conditions would be like for a swim.

Ferrying

Ferrying is a technique used to cross current laterally without drifting downstream. In a ferry, you point the upstream end of the kayak (which is your bow if you are facing upstream, or your stern if you are facing downstream) on an angle to the current. The current is deflected off the leading end of the kayak, creating a lateral force that assists with the kayak's movement across the current. Too little angle between the kayak and the current means that you're paddling straight upstream against the current's force. Too much angle means you are turning broadside to the current and the kayak is getting pushed downstream. Remember, current is current whether it is caused by gravity in a river or the gravitational pull of the moon, as with tides in the ocean. Also, it is helpful to know that the principle of ferrying works when you are crossing from one side of a channel to another in a really strong wind — think of the wind as a flow of water and angle your kayak accordingly.

SAFETY TIP
Wear a paddling helmet and paddle with a buddy whenever you are on moving water or in surf.

1 FERRYING Set up the angle of your kayak in relation to the current; this angle needs to be great enough to carry you sideways, but not so great that your bow gets spun downstream. The stronger the current, the smaller the angle, and the gentler the current, the greater the angle.

2 Establish speed in the eddy before crossing the line using the power forward. Edge your kayak downstream as you cross this unstable water; otherwise, you will spin around and get pushed back into the eddy or flip over.

3 It takes some practice to maintain your ferry angle so that you don't get spun downstream. Paddle across the current with the kayak on edge.

4 Focus on your destination. By doing this, your body will find its balance and you will intuitively take the kayak in the right direction.

5 It is important to edge your kayak in the direction of the turn. You can use a reverse sweeping low brace as shown here.

6 The kayaker is poised at the top of the eddy, ready to either continue downstream or peel out and ferry back across the current.

Peeling Out

At some point, you will need to cross an eddy line, either to get into an eddy or to get out of one. The narrowest part of the eddy line is at the place where it passes the obstruction, so you want to leave an eddy up near the obstacle. Cross the eddy line with speed, edging your kayak downstream and angling you kayak correctly to the current. We find the acronym SEA (think of sea kayak) is an easy way to remember the key ingredients to leaving and entering eddies: **SPEED, EDGE, ANGLE.** In order to be in control you need to be traveling faster than the leaving current, you need to be edging in the direction in which you are turning, and you must be angled correctly to the current. Edging your kayak is particularly important or else the current will catch your upstream edge and very quickly flip you upstream.

The main point of this maneuver is to carve a smooth arcing turn completely across the eddy line, maintaining forward momentum throughout. The demonstration photographed here is taking place in simple current without obstacles where there is a clearly defined eddy line. It is important to cross eddy lines with strong intent because the eddy line itself is unstable and unpredictable.

If you are a coastal kayaker, you will undoubtedly encounter these conditions regularly, especially if you paddle where there are tides. The same skills useful in whitewater river paddling, particularly the angling and edging of the kayak, can also be applied to paddling across a channel in a strong wind. A tidal stream is often not as neatly contained as a river is by banks that define the mainstream and the eddies, and the scale is often considerably larger than that of a river. However, as a tidal stream rushes around an island or headland, its behavior is the same as that of a river. If you kayak in river current, you will find understanding what tides are doing to the sea a lot less complicated.

1 **PEELING OUT** Leaving an eddy and heading downstream is known as peeling out. This large eddy makes it easier for the novice kayaker to get the boat angled properly and have enough forward momentum to quickly cross the unstable water of the eddy line.

2 Just before you cross the eddy line, use a forward sweep to initiate the turn just as in the low brace U-turn. This will assist the current in spinning the bow around to face downstream.

3 As you cross the eddy line, edge the kayak downstream by rotating your torso to face downstream. Initiate a reverse sweeping low brace on the downstream side of the kayak.

4 J-lean. Continue edging into the turn using the reverse sweeping low brace.

5 Your blade needs to sweep forward to a point directly out to the side from your hip. There should be a climbing angle on the blade so that it provides both support and turning power. Your kayak is actually turning around this low brace.

6 In a smooth transition, follow up the low brace with strong forward strokes and continue on downstream.

Surfing

To the initiated, the surf zone is a really fun place to paddle. Never mind that the temperatures may require donning a drysuit, you look forward eagerly to the thrill just as a river paddler is excited by the challenge of whitewater. The surf zone is a training ground that can hone your skills in a variety of conditions and scenarios. Instead of letting the water's power intimidate you, learn how to play with it. There is no better place to improve your strokes, rescues and capsize recoveries, and your overall knowledge of wind and water.

If you ever paddle on an open coastline, you need to know how to handle landing and launching in surf. The weather can change, and injury or other events can necessitate an unexpected landing. That being said, the power of fast-moving, rolling water, especially as it meets a coastline, can cause serious injury to people who are unprepared and experienced.

Stern Ruddering Strokes

Stern ruddering strokes are the most powerful means to steer the kayak while moving forward without losing speed. They are also important strokes to use for minor course corrections while surfing waves. There are two ruddering strokes; the stern draw and the stern pry. The stern draw draws the stern to the paddle. But since pushing is a more powerful action than pulling, the most powerful stern ruddering stroke is the stern pry. in which you plant the paddle at the stern and, using the back face of the paddle, push the kayak away from the blade. With a kayak paddle, the stern draw on one side is merely the stern pry on the other. Most of the time while surfing, kayakers simply alternate side to side with stern pries.

To use a stern ruddering stroke as a strong corrective measure, you can incorporate it into your forward stroke. Continue the forward stroke past your hip. Keep rotating your torso so your hands are in front of your body. Paddling within the Paddler's Box while in surf is particularly important in order to prevent shoulder injuries and dislocations. Your top hand drops down until the paddle shaft is parallel to your kayak. The blade is fully submerged and vertical for maximum effect. One thing to keep in mind is that this offers very little support unless you adjust the pitch of the blade to provide some bracing.

To better understand why ruddering strokes are so powerful, return to Chapter 6 and review Physical Resistances That Affect a Kayak. When

Stern ruddering strokes are an effective way to make slight course corrections while surfing.

the water flows past the widest part of the hull, a vacuum is left in the spaces along either side of the stern. These spaces are essentially eddies and they are filled with unstable swirling water. At the following end of the kayak, you find the least amount of pressure on the hull. This allows the stern to swing more freely from side to side than the leading end (the bow). Strokes made in this end of the kayak have the greatest effect.

A CHECKLIST FOR PROTECTING YOURSELF WHILE SURFING WAVES

- Wear a helmet.
- Double-check that everything on your deck is very secure.
- Have a strong, consistent roll.
- Protect your shoulders from injury by keeping your arms within the Paddler's Box and your elbows low and close to your body.
- Keep seaward of your kayak when assisting, swimming and getting in or out.
- Know the surf riding rules, and land and launch one at a time to avoid collisions.

OPPOSITE Rocketing down the face of a wave, small or large, is a thrilling ride on nature's waterslide.

1 **SURFING A WAVE** Look back over your shoulder to watch for the kind of wave you want to catch. It may be that you are waiting for a smaller wave to land on shore, or perhaps you are hoping for a larger wave to ride. (Novices can practice surfing techniques in gentle swells.)

2 Catching the wave requires timing and speed. Line yourself up perpendicular to the oncoming wave and power forward aggressively just before it reaches you.

3 As your stern is lifted on the wave, you can stop paddling, as gravity will hold you there on the face of the wave. Control your run with stern ruddering strokes.

4 The bow will likely dive, or purl, deflecting either left or right. Instead of fighting this, edge into (not away from) the wave.

5 Ride the break using a high or low brace, hold the speed and carve off it. Continue edging your kayak to the inside of the turn. As the wave breaks, you will run parallel with it. Continue to use a low or high brace, edging and bracing into the wave.

6 Keep your arms tucked in close to your body and keep your torso within the all-important Paddler's Box throughout the entire surfing ride. Continue to hold the brace, allowing it to act as the pivot point around which the kayak is turning in order to head back out for another run. (This is the U-turn maneuver.)

Pitchpoling

If you are surfing a wave that continues to steepen, there comes a point when the bow will begin to purl, or bury itself in the bottom of the wave. This has the effect of arresting forward momentum at the bow while still pushing the stern forward until the kayak is in an upright position. This is called pitchpoling, otherwise known as doing an ender or a loop. A skilled paddler can do different things from this position — from pole vaulting (when the kayak touches the bottom) to the challenging pirouette, where the paddler actually spins the vertical kayak around on its bow before it falls back to the surface.

CHAPTER 9

SAFETY AND RESCUE GEAR

ONCE THE SNOW STARTS MELTING and ski and snowshoe travel become impractical, we know the paddling season will soon be upon us. It is an exciting time as rivers swell with spring melt fanning out at the edges of shore, and house-sized hummocks of ice break off crashing into the lake. Gulls perching at the edge of the ice floes fish in the bay whose blue waters have been hidden from us for four long months. Early spring is the time when we get our kayaking gear ready for the first day on the water. We pull the kayaks out of the barn and lay them in the snow to inspect decklines and rudder cables, skeg boxes and carrying toggles to make sure everything is in good working order. This is also the time we get all our paddling gear together, including the four things legally required while kayaking on Canadian waters — a PFD, bailer, 15 m floating rope, sound signaling device and a waterproof flashlight.

In the following few pages, we'll describe the items not already covered in Chapter 2, The Outfit. Techniques for using pumps and paddle floats, and maps, charts and compasses are covered in the next two chapters. Although there is a plethora of great gear that can make kayaking safer and more comfortable, the most important things to have will always be the skills, knowledge and good judgment you gain only through experience.

OPPOSITE It is only when night falls that we realize the sky is not blue at all but merely reflected light.

RIGHT More than a thousand years ago, the Vikings arrived in the deep fjords of southwest Greenland. Eventually they surrendered their small farms to the harsh climate, leaving little more than sod foundations and lonely graves.

Essentials Checklist

- PFD (personal floatation device)
- Sprayskirt
- Hat and spare clothes (windproof dry top, fleece jacket) in a waterproof dry bag
- Bilge pump and sponge
- Paddle float and rescue sling
- 50-foot (15 m) floating rope in throwbag or towing belt
- Signaling kit, whistle and waterproof flashlight
- Repair kit
- First-aid kit
- Water bottle and energy bars
- Spare paddle
- Handheld compass, chart case and VHF radio

TIP A paddle leash is handy little item for keeping paddler and paddle together, or kayak and paddle attached, especially in the event of a capsize, or to keep a young kayaker's dropped paddle from floating away.

BILGE PUMP AND SPONGE

After recovering from a capsize, you need some way of getting the water out of the cockpit. The bilge pump is the most effective method of emptying a flooded cockpit. The most popular ones are handheld because they are simple to use, reliable and can be shared. We each keep one securely attached under the bungees on the kayak foredeck so that it is always handy. These hand-operated ones work well despite a couple of drawbacks. You need both hands available to pump, yet the conditions which may have caused the capsize in the first place are undoubtedly going to make it hard to pump and balance in a kayak that is still full of water. It is certainly helpful to have assistance if you are pumping out a kayak. You can take turns pumping and stabilizing the two kayaks. The other challenge is that you need to slip the pump into the hull through the upturned edge of the sprayskirt, which can potentially allow water to slosh back in. Your handheld pump needs a brightly colored floating collar so you can see it and it won't sink.

Other options are a foot-operated bilge pump, deck-mounted hand pump, or an electric pump kept in good running order. A boat sponge is handy for mopping up water, sand and mud. Keeping a tidy ship ensures that any moving parts such as the rudder and adjustable foot braces work properly.

Carrying a spare paddle is just good insurance against a ferrule jamming or a shaft breaking. Also it can be useful to have two different paddles depending on the type of excursion on which you are embarking. For instance, it can be nice to have a shorter, wider-bladed, less expensive paddle for surfing.

PADDLE FLOATS, SPONSONS AND RESCUE SLINGS

For a solo paddler who is practiced in the use of these devices, they can prove life-saving. The paddle floats and rescue slings enable a paddler to reenter his kayak from the water without help from anyone else. And they can also greatly assist a group of paddlers as well. The sponsons are useful in certain situations to prevent capsizing.

A paddle float is flotation that is attached to a paddle blade to give you support while you reenter your kayak from the water. Of the two paddle floats shown here, one is the more common inflatable sort, and the other solid foam type is ideal for a solo day paddler who does not know how to roll. The solid foam one is particularly useful in cold water conditions where a person needs to get out of the water as quickly as possible. A paddle float needs to provide adequate flotation for a heavy person, and you must be able to secure it to the paddle blade.

Inflatable sponsons attach to either side of your kayak, acting as outriggers to stabilize it. Since they clip into deck hardware, you need to rig a kayak for them before going paddling. They are useful for towing a seasick or injured paddler, and can be used as "training wheels" for an unsteady paddler.

A rescue sling is a length of floating rope or webbing that forms a loop. This loop is handy during a capsize recovery when the person in the water needs assistance climbing from the water into the kayak. The sling can be used in both solo and assisted recoveries. Premade adjustable webbing loops can be fashioned from a length of 5/16-to-3/8-inch (8–9 mm) line, about 13 feet (4 m) long, which forms the loop by way of a double fisherman's knot. I prefer to use an adjustable webbing loop, which I carry in one of my PFD pockets or under the bungees on the deck of my kayak.

An adjustable webbing rescue sling.

An inflatable paddle float and a rigid, closed-cell foam paddle float.

Sponsons are installed by means of straps wrapped around the hull fore and aft of the cockpit coaming. These straps should be adjusted to fit the kayak before leaving shore. The sponsons can be inflated immediately or as needed.

Sponsons provide enough stability to allow an agile paddler to stand in the kayak.

TOWING EQUIPMENT

Towing equipment is becoming standard gear on any paddling trip. A towing system consists of a length of rope, a carabineer to attach the leash to the kayak being towed, and a quick-release buckle for the rescuer to disconnect himself quickly from the towline. Tow ropes must float. They are carried in a pouch on the back of the PFD, around a paddler's waist, or attached to the kayak. A non-corrosive carabineer is used to attach the towline to the kayak needing assistance. For the safety of the person doing the towing, proper tow ropes feature a quick-release that enables a rescuer to release themselves from the tow with a flick of the wrist. The ones shown here include a quick-release waist belt and a quick-release cockpit coaming loop. Towlines often include a length of bungee to absorb the constant jerking that occurs between the kayak doing the pulling and the one being pulled. A kayaker's towlines vary in length from 3 to 50 feet (1–15 m). The greater length of rope is necessary so the kayak being towed does not ram its bow into the stern end of the rescuer's kayak. One of the most common ways of using this tow is in a simple in-line tow to assist a tired or injured paddler. A long rope can be shortened in a neat fashion called a daisy chain (see Chapter 14, Tying It All Together). A pigtail or cowtail towline can be as short as 3 feet (1 m). It is handy for corraling an empty kayak during an assisted reentry, stabilizing a towed paddler, or towing a kayak over a short distance.

The back view of the PFD shows the quick-release waist belt. Here the PFD is shown with a pigtail towline attached to the D-ring on the back of the PFD. When the waist belt of the PFD is released, this towline separates instantly from the PFD.

This pigtail towline is dual purpose in that it can instantly be extended from a short pigtail into a longer towline in order to provide distance between your kayak and the one being towed.

WAIST-BELT TOWLINE A length of bungee cord is set into the towing rope to provide flex to help absorb the jerking of the towed kayak.

A long towline is generally carried in a waist pouch. The 50 feet (15 m) of daisy-chained rope is easily made shorter or longer, depending on the use intended.

A more compact waist-belt towline with an easy to grab quick-release (the little red ball), so you don't have to fumble for the buckle.

There are 25 feet (7.5m) of floating rope stored in this compact waist-belt towline pouch.

COAMING TOW ROPE This towline attaches to the cockpit coaming with an adjustable loop instead of your waist, making it more comfortable for longer tows. The clasp on the end of the throwbag is attached to the kayak being towed.

When the rubber knob is pulled, the gate on the brass clasp opens, releasing the nylon ring and disconnecting the circle of rope around the cockpit of the towing kayak.

FLOTATION BAGS

It was May just after the ice had gone out and we were camped in the Rossport Islands on Lake Superior's north shore. There was a slight breeze blowing off the land out into the lake but the air was bright and warm. Gary saw what looked like a yellow marker buoy in the bay, but once he looked through his binoculars, he could see it was the bow of a kayak bobbing in the bay with a man hanging onto it. By the time Gary had paddled out to him, the fellow, who was poorly dressed for the situation, was well into the first stages of hypothermia. He was shaking uncontrollably and his poor little dog, who had been trying desperately to scramble onto the slippery, overturned hull, now attempted to climb onto Gary's kayak.

After quickly assessing the situation, Gary knew that the most urgent matter was to get this person and his dog out of the water. The man clutched onto the dog and hauled himself onto Gary's back deck. Gary paddled for shore as fast as could, got a fire lit and helped him into dry clothes. Then Gary returned to the kayak, which was now sinking. All that was keeping it afloat was the trapped air in the bow. He realized that the man had left the cover off his back hatch in order to provide his dog with a place to sit. Kayaks that do not have sealed bulkheads must have flotation bags. He had effectively taken away the inherent flotation feature that the stern sealed bulkhead provided. To make matters worse, the bow did not have a sealed bulkhead, nor did it have any additional flotation. Luckily, when the

This view of a collapsible kayak frame shows exactly where the stern flotation bag goes. Kayaks that do not have sealed bulkheads must have flotation bags to provide flotation.

man tipped over, the stern end quickly filled with water, upending the kayak so the bow appeared as a vertical beacon. Without the trapped air in the bow, the kayak would undoubtedly have sunk. Gary found the water-filled kayak difficult to empty but he eventually got it up on his deck and the water drained out. Suffice to say, the fellow probably would have succumbed to hypothermia and then drowned if it were not for Gary's quick response. If you do take a hatch cover off for some reason, be sure to fill the end of the kayak with a flotation bag.

FIRST-AID KIT

We are far safer traveling in our kayaks than we ever are zooming down the highway. However, whenever we go out onto the water, especially into remote wilderness settings, we have a responsibility to ourselves, and others if we are guiding, to be able to deal with first-aid concerns such as blisters, chafing, rashes, tendonitis, carpal tunnel syndrome, kayaker's elbow, sunburn, seasickness, cuts, stings, infections, dehydration, hypothermia and hyperthermia. Prevention and common sense are the keys to avoiding these maladies.

We have two first-aid kits. One is a small kit that gets thrown in any time we go on a day hike, an afternoon paddle or a moonlight ski. It is packed and ready to go, and it includes the basics for taking care of cuts, blisters and headaches. The other kit is for wilderness expeditions, and its contents address many more scenarios where professional help may be hours or days away. Knowing how to use the materials in your first-aid kit, and having the wherewithal to deal with a variety of situations is something one carries in one's head through experience and personal character. Consider taking a wilderness first-aid training course.

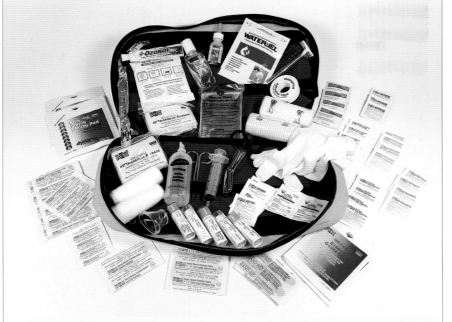

FIRST-AID KIT: DAYTRIPPING KIT

- Adhesive bandages of all sizes and shapes
- Moleskin for blisters
- Cloth tape (1/2 to 1 inch)
- Scissors
- Safety pins
- Tweezers
- Pure aloe vera gel for burns
- Tincture of benzoin (cleans damp and dirty skin so that adhesive bandages will stick)
- Eye bath

EXPEDITION KIT (add to the above)

- Pressure dressing
- Triangular bandages
- Sterile gauze
- 3M breathable wound dressing

- Crepe wrap
- Pain relief (aspirin, ibuprofen, acetaminophen)
- Antinausea medication
- Antidiarrhea medication
- Antihistamine
- Personal medications
- Echinacea for sore throat

We also carry some excellent homeopathic remedies:

- Rescue Remedy for calming a panicky person or animal that is frightened or in pain
- Apis for bee stings
- Arnica for bruising
- Belladona for fever and too much sun
- Ginger for calming the stomach

REPAIR KIT

- Cord
- Vinyl repair kit for airbags and inflatable sleeping pads
- Pliers and screwdrivers to match nuts and bolts on all kayaks
- Small vise-grip pliers
- Multi-tool
- Extra nuts and bolts and waterproof washers
- Extra rudder or skeg cable
- Neoprene and nylon patches with AquaSeal adhesive
- Waterproof tape (such as duct tape)
- Stove parts
- Extra Swiss army knife

- Sharpening stone
- Tent pole sleeve
- Needle and thread to mend clothing, etc.
- Urethane adhesive
- Two-part epoxy
- Narrow-gauge wire
- Shoe Goo to repair footwear
- Fiberglass repair kit
- Spare gaskets for drysuits
- Assortment of Fastex buckles to fix hatch straps
- Spring button replacement for take-apart paddle
- Nylon cable ties

Signaling Devices

These devices are used to attract attention, either of fellow paddlers, or of a search and rescue team. Whistles, waterproof flashlights and paddles are the simplest to use and can attract the attention of someone close by. However, if you are involved in a rescue situation where outside assistance is needed, the correct signaling device can make a big difference in pinpointing your location to an aircraft. You should always know where you are and how to describe your position on your map and on a GPS unit to a rescue party by way of a VHF radio. Depending on when and where a paddler travels, it may be a good idea to carry both sound and visual devices for day and night use. The array of signaling devices shown here are for use in emergency rescues only. If you have the opportunity to attend a search-and-rescue training session, you can see for yourself the effectiveness of flares. While smoke and dye are useful during the day, flares are more easily observed at night. Flares are potentially dangerous and need to be handled, carried and stored with care.

FLARES

Flares range from pencil flares to parachute flares to a pistol flare gun. These work best in the dark. Dye, smoke and mirrors are best used in the daytime. Small smoke canisters set off a billowing cloud of orange smoke. On a windy day, the smoke disappears quickly. Dye markers secrete an orange or green nontoxic substance into the water that can be seen from a high vantage point such as an aircraft. Dye is used to mark your position when someone is already

TOP ROW, LEFT TO RIGHT Smoke flare, glow sticks, manual air horn, pea-less whistle, signaling mirror, parachute flare, VHF radio, cell phone.
BOTTOM ROW, LEFT TO RIGHT Orange flag, twin rocket flare, red and orange handheld flares, handheld bright incendiary flare, waterproof container for matches, pistol flare gun, extra flares, a reusable pocket flare and a disposable pocket flare.

looking for you. A signaling mirror turned to reflect sunlight can be used to attract attention. Some people like carrying their flares in their PFDs but we feel a fair bit of anxiety about attaching an arsenal to ourselves and would rather have an easily accessible kit behind our seat. Dispose of expired flares responsibly at your local fire department.

STROBES

A waterproof strobe can be attached to your PFD or your kayak. Activating this bright white, flashing light is a means of signaling for help. But it is also (and more often, we hope) an effective way of marking your position on the water to fellow paddlers if you are traveling at night. It is important, as with all your equipment, to keep strobes in good running order with silicon grease on the O-ring and fresh charged batteries.

FLASHLIGHT

A waterproof flashlight is a necessary piece of equipment for a late day or overnight adventure. After sunset, the Coast Guard requires that you carry a white light so you can be seen and identified as a human-powered vessel. We wear waterproof headlamps, as they free our hands and are useful once we come ashore.

SOUND SIGNALS

On the water, the sound of waves and wind will overwhelm your voice no matter how loud you can yell. We have already noted that a rescue whistle (the pea-less kind) should be attached to your PFD. But even a whistle doesn't carry far against the wind. A manual air horn is much louder and useful if you want to be heard in the fog wherever there is boat traffic.

VHF RADIOS AND CELL AND SATELLITE PHONES

We traveled for years without relying on these devices because they simply weren't available. We were forced to be responsible for rescuing

A waterproof VHF radio, which also acts as a weather radio, and a cell phone, along with waterproof cases to carry them. Trapped air and foam in the waterproof cases provide buoyancy to keep them afloat.

ourselves, watching the weather signs and planning ahead. Today we strive to maintain this attitude. Electronic devices are wonderful tools for instructors and guides, and indeed traveling without some kind of radio communication would be considered irresponsible when you have people depending on you. We use our VHF radio all the time to listen to the local weather broadcast. There are also marine-operator channels for communication with other vessels, marinas or land lines. But most important, you can put out a distress call on Channel 16, the emergency channel, which is monitored by the

Coast Guard and other boats in the area. This channel is kept open and used only for emergencies. If you are in a busy boating area, it is advisable to carry your VHF radio in a handy place ready to use. When you purchase it, you should get instructions on its use and in registering a call name. (In many jurisdictions, this is legally required.) Using a VHF is a simple process, but to be safe and courteous, you must learn the operating rules. Always protect your VHF radio in a waterproof case.

Cell phones can be carried as a communication device but if you are relying on one for emergency use, check to make sure that there is cell service where you are paddling. Also it may be a good idea to talk with your paddling partners beforehand to agree on the protocol of cell phone use while on the water.

We have been using satellite phones on wilderness journeys since 1997. Although our purpose has been for the broadcast of radio interviews and the transmission of photographs and written stories for various media and the internet, we have come to respect the advantages of this form of communication, if used sensibly. In our Arctic travels, a satellite phone has been very helpful in pinpointing and describing our exact pickup location to an aircraft. We have also heard stories of medical emergencies where having the use of a satellite phone has meant the difference between life and death.

CAPSIZE RECOVERIES AND RESCUES

One of the biggest challenges facing you anytime you step into your kayak and paddle away from shore, whether alone or in the company of others, is the possibility of an unexpected capsize. There can be a lot of fear associated with this anticipated experience. At some point, you are going to tip over in your kayak. It is good to accept this and get the experience under your belt as soon as possible. You can't commit to a brace, or edge or J-lean the kayak, or even rotate your torso with any vigor if you are constantly worried about tipping.

For many novices, the notion that you will be stuck in the cockpit upside down underwater is a very real fear. You need to get past this feeling if you are going to enjoy kayaking. If you are comfortable in the water, you are comfortable on the water, so spending time in the water is important. When we were young we spent hours and hours in the summer playing around with kayaks on a lake with warm water and a shallow sandy bottom. We would get in them, turn them over, spin each other around upside down, and try rolling using the dock or each other's bow.

Also, it is a really good idea to start out with some instruction. You can learn rescue techniques in the winter months, as many kayak instructors take advantage of the local indoor pool to offer rolling clinics and capsize recovery workshops. The more time you spend getting in and out of your kayak, the more confidence you will gain.

A Word About the Demonstrations

A capsized paddler needs to get upright and be on her way again. Doing this without aid from another paddler is called a self-rescue. Because a paddler should learn to be self-reliant whether alone or in the company of others, we will begin with these recoveries. If you are unable to roll, you will have to get back in the kayak, get the water out of the kayak and make sure that you are steady before setting off again. At other times, the situation requires that you receive or give assistance to get out of a dangerous or harmful situation. There are any number of ways to get a capsized kayaker upright and no one method is the best. It depends on the judgment, skill and physical capabilities of the people involved, the wind and water conditions and the equipment, but it is safe to say that the methods that are consistently reliable for you are the best techniques for you to use.

The demonstrations shown here were performed in optimum conditions for the benefit of the reader, to see what is being accomplished.

A poorly timed return to a steep beach resulted in an unexpected but exciting ride.

Coming in on the surf at day's end, Sea of Cortez.

Chances are high that when you need to use a recovery, conditions are going to be windy and or rough, and the circumstances are often unexpected. In order to carry out these capsize recoveries and rescues effectively, you need to practice them in the kinds of conditions. You will find, with experience, that a wide variety of scenarios are cause for capsize. Having a repertoire of well-rehearsed recoveries to draw upon can be life saving. Remember, in a life-threatening situation, your body needs to go on automatic pilot, and that happens only if you have trained yourself in the response to take.

We are going to look at a number of solo recoveries followed by assisted recoveries and rescues, but first we are going to look at the wet exit, and then the roll — the simplest and most effective recovery. Any recovery that involves a swimmer is more complex. Many factors compound the situation and will affect how you decide to proceed — the swimmer's safety, the loss of equipment, keeping track of other kayakers in a group, as well as the amount of time that is taken up in getting someone back into a kayak, pumping the water out and fully stabilizing this possibly cold, wet person so that you can carry on.

The Wet Exit

It is important to have the experience of a wet exit so you are confident and comfortable getting out of the kayak while upside down underwater. The wet exit is also the beginning of a further self or assisted rescue. Start with a dry land run. Sit in the kayak, put on the sprayskirt and make sure the grab loop is easy to reach. Pretend you have tipped over. Lean forward, take hold of the grab loop and pull it forward to release it from the coaming. Then pull it back. Slide your hands along the coaming to release the edge of the skirt.

If you are at all nervous, choose a place with as close to ideal conditions for your first wet exit. If you can find it, a gently sloping sandy bottom where the water is warm and clear is perfect. Calm, comfortable weather will make your first efforts easier. (If you are really worried about the sprayskirt, just do your first wet exit without a sprayskirt on.) Consider wearing a scuba diving mask to help you to see what you are doing — at the very least, a pair of noseplugs will help you avoid a rush of water up your nose.

Once you are in the kayak on the water, you are ready to begin. Hang on to your paddle. Take a deep breath and stay calm. Lift one knee and tip the kayak over. Take a moment to orient yourself (this is where the scuba mask comes in handy). Lean forward and reach for the spray-skirt grab loop. Pull it forward and away from the coaming. Relax your legs so they fall away from the thigh braces. With hands on either side of the coaming, push yourself out of the kayak, although in truth, you really just fall out of the kayak at this point (unless you are tightly wedged into one that is too small for you).

When you surface beside the kayak, you will realize that all of this took far less than 10 seconds! Hang on to your kayak and your paddle. If you tip unexpectedly in a wind, hang on to your kayak and paddle. On one wave, they can get away from you faster than you can swim. If you are alone and this happens, you are in serious trouble. Once you are in the water, holding your paddle and kayak, there are all kinds of ways that you can get back in your kayak, but first we are going to consider the roll.

The tens of thousands of lakes and rivers around the Great Lakes coast make it one of the best paddling destinations in the world.

Rolling Your Kayak

Rolling your kayak is the ultimate self-rescue. You tip over but then you are able to right yourself while keeping the inside of your kayak and your lower body completely dry! It is not only the simplest, fastest and most effective rescue technique; it is also a skill that has been essential to the tradition of kayaking dating back thousands of years. An Arctic Ocean capsize would nearly always have meant death by drowning or hypothermia for any Inuit paddler unable to roll. Whether you are paddling in an ice-cold ocean or on a balmy cottage lake, being able to roll a kayak allows you the freedom to push your limits. Almost any reasonably fit person can roll a kayak, as it relies on technique not muscle. Even a loaded kayak means merely an adjustment in timing, as it rolls slower than an empty one.

Practicing your rolls in all kinds of conditions is the key to becoming a proficient roller. When you are not on the water, try using the visualization technique discussed in Chapter 4, Balancing the Body. Picture and feel yourself successfully accomplishing the roll, remaining calm and methodical each step of the way.

Learning to roll is best accomplished in the company of a good instructor. If you develop the correct technique from the beginning, you won't get discouraged. That being said, there are people who will never be physically capable of learning to roll, lack of flexibility being one reason. A person unable to roll can enjoy kayaking as much as the next person but strong self-rescue skills are a must, especially if you paddle alone.

1 C TO C ROLL Establish the set-up position before capsizing. Lean forward. Lay the paddle alongside you with your knuckles down. The blade forward will have the power face up and on the same plane as the hull, turned slightly out.

2 Tip over by lifting your opposite knee. It takes a moment for the kayak to capsize. Feel your hands pushing the blade to the surface. If your power face is correct on the set-up, it will face down and be on a climbing angle.

3 Start sweeping across the surface out to the side of the kayak, keeping the blade at the surface until the paddle is perpendicular—90 degrees—with the kayak.

4 Pull down on the paddle to provide temporary support. (Note that the blade does not dive down.) This is the catch and it is at this moment that you aggressively hip snap. This is the leverage that rights the kayak. Keep your top arm, the pivot arm, tucked in.

5 Keep your head against your low shoulder so that it is the last thing to come up. During the roll, the hip snap quickly pulling the kayak underneath you forms the second "C" in the C to C roll.

Learning to Roll: The Phases

There are dozens of ways to roll your kayak. Common to the C to C roll and sweep roll demonstrated here are three phases. The set-up gets you into the correct position to begin the roll. (When you are learning, you can assume this set-up position before you even tip over.) Then there is the catch, when you are using your paddle, hands or a float on the water surface to support your upper body. Finally, in the recovery phase, your knee lift and hip snap brings the kayak underneath you to sit upright again.

The knee lift and hip snap requires timing between your upper and lower body. It refers particularly to the action of rotating your hips to bring the kayak upright and underneath you. It is the most important element in learning to roll. Maintain the Paddler's Box position throughout with your arms in front of your body to protect your shoulder from injury. This means that your upper body must rotate independently of your lower body.

TIP THE SELF-RESCUE ATTITUDE

Be responsible for yourself on the water even if you are with others. You greatly increase your own and other people's safety. If you wet exit, use self-rescue techniques to get back in the kayak as quickly as possible.

1 SWEEP ROLL Establish the set-up position before capsizing. Lay the paddle alongside you with your knuckles down. The blade forward will have the power face up and on the same plane as the hull, turned slightly out.

2 Tip over by lifting your opposite knee. It takes a moment for the kayak to capsize. Feel your hands pushing the blade through the surface. If your power face is correct on the set-up, it will face down and be on a climbing angle. This is very important.

3 Start sweeping across the surface applying downward pressure. Keep the blade at the surface maintaining the climbing angle.

4 Let your head follow the active blade during the sweep. Use your knee (right one in this case) to lift up and hip snap to roll the kayak upright.

5 Keep your head low. It is the last thing to come up once the kayak is upright. Remember to keep your arms within the Paddler's Box to protect your shoulder from injury.

Rolling a Tandem Kayak

Rolling a tandem kayak requires the same technique as rolling solo, however you must now coordinate the set-up, the catch and most especially the knee lift and hip snap with your partner. Remember as you practice the hip snap that you are lifting the lower knee and pressing the opposite buttock into the seat in order to pull the kayak underneath you. The kayak's larger size inherently makes it a slower boat to roll and your timing must reflect this or your body comes up faster than the kayak. A smaller paddler has to work harder to hold herself in position in the larger cockpit. A fully loaded tandem kayak is a very stable craft, so much so that it is unlikely you are going to accidentally tip one. We look upon mastering the tandem roll as a confidence-building challenge.

Paddling a tandem kayak requires teamwork, a rhythm suited to both people, and a sense of humor. As in any wilderness voyage, the challenge of difficult weather is not nearly as critical as maintaining friendly relationships between comrades.

1 **TANDEM ROLL** Set up as in the solo roll. Lay the paddle alongside you with your knuckles down. The blade forward will have the power face up and on the same plane as the hull, turned slightly out. Lift up with your outside knees to capsize the kayak.

2 Take time to let the kayak get all the way over. Both paddlers must allow their hands and paddles to break the surface.

3 As you begin to apply pressure with your blades on the surface, this is the catch phase of the sweep.

4 In unison, sweep out to the side of the kayak, applying steady downward pressure. Keep the blades at the surface, maintaining the climbing angle.

5 Watch your active blade as you move it across the surface during the sweep and hip snap.

6 Both paddlers need to keep their heads as low as possible, bringing them up only at the very last. A coordinated effort is key to the success of the tandem roll.

The Scramble

If you possess the balance and agility, the scramble is the quickest self-rescue method for getting out of the water and back into the kayak. This recovery works best if you are on calm waters and a companion comes to your aid to stabilize the kayak while you pump it out, or if you have an automatic bailer that can leave your hands free to maintain balance in your unsteady flooded cockpit.

Waves of sand ripple down to the sea where gray whales gather to take shelter in this age-old calving bay.

1 **THE SCRAMBLE** Hold on to your kayak and your paddle. Grab the cockpit coaming and flip the kayak upright.

2 Reach across the cockpit, float your feet close to the surface and use strong scissor kicks to swim yourself onto the stern.

3 Keeping your body low for stability, swing your leg over the stern.

4 Straddle the kayak as if you are riding a horse. Make sure the front of your sprayskirt is out in front of you so that as you slide forward, it doesn't get caught underneath you.

5 Now comes the tricky balancing part — getting your legs into the cockpit. Be ready to use a sculling brace for support as you drop your bottom into the seat and then bring your legs in one after the other. Fasten the sprayskirt and pump the water out.

6 Once you are in the kayak, partially fasten the sprayskirt, leaving an opening for the pump. Pump the water out of the cockpit, then secure the pump and make sure the sprayskirt is completely attached to the kayak.

Paddle Float Outrigger

An inflatable paddle float provides stability on one side of the kayak as you reenter the cockpit. This piece of equipment works best in relatively calm conditions. There are any number of variations on its use but they all must be practiced if they are to be effective recoveries in time of need.

1 RECOVERY WITH PADDLE FLOAT OUTRIGGER
Hold on to your kayak and paddle.

2 Grab the coaming and flip the kayak over. Take your paddle float from under the bungee on the bow deck.

6 Remove your foot from the cockpit and place the paddle across the back deck, clamping the paddle shaft and cockpit coaming securely together. Float your legs, then kick and swim onto the cockpit.

7 Hook your foot (nearest the stern) onto the shaft of the paddle near the float once you are out of the water. Twist to face the stern.

8 Swing the leg nearest the bow into the cockpit. Keep your weight low and balanced over the paddle float side of the kayak. (It helps to keep an eye on the float.)

3 Slip one leg into the cockpit to hold the kayak. You need both hands to attach and use the paddle float.

4 Place the float on one blade, then wrap the strap around the paddle shaft and fasten the quick-release buckle to ensure you won't lose the float. You will be placing a fair amount of weight on it.

5 Inflate the paddle float.

9 Once seated, bring the paddle forward and use it as a brace while you secure your sprayskirt, pump out the water and deflate the paddle float.

1 **DEFLATING FLOAT** Open the valve on the paddle float and keep it above the surface.

2 Force the inflated paddle float underwater, allowing the water pressure to compress the float. Close the valve, unfasten the strap and store the float where it is secure yet accessible.

Reenter and Roll

If your roll fails and you find yourself wet exiting, there is another way to reenter the flooded cockpit. Take a deep breath, climb back into the overturned kayak and set up another roll. The challenge is to remain upright in the flooded cockpit while you pump out. Take a few moments to attach the paddle float before attempting your reenter and roll. Once you are upright, the outrigger gives you much more stability for emptying out the cockpit.

Paddling with icebergs is traveling among unpredictable giants, some resembling dinosaurs and dragons.

1 **SOLO REENTRY AND ROLL** Keep hold of your kayak while securing and inflating the paddle float on your paddle. Lift the edge of the cockpit and slide your legs into the cockpit.

2 Take a deep breath and slide the rest of the way into the cockpit.

3 Get your bottom properly in the seat and get a good grip with your knees and thighs on the thigh braces. Set up the roll as in the solo sweep roll described earlier.

4 Sweep out to the side maintaining downward pressure on the blade as you simultaneously perform the righting action with your hips and knees.

5 Keep your head low until you are all the way up.

6 A sweep roll or extended paddle roll works best for the reentry and roll because the kayak is full of water and you come up fairly slowly.

Face-up Recoveries

In this recovery, the swimmer uses either her own righted kayak with paddle and paddle float, or her own righted kayak and the rescuer's kayak as support. In a feet-first, face-up orientation, an agile swimmer can quickly reenter the cockpit with the advantage of facing forward. Arch your back, keep your head back and swing your legs up and into the cockpit.

1 FACE-UP SOLO RECOVERY Flip the kayak upright. Set up the outrigger. Facing the bow, stretch one arm out along the shaft and the other arm over the stern of the kayak behind the seat.

2 Kick one leg into the cockpit and then the other.

3 Slide your legs into the cockpit. Maintain pressure on the outrigger while you reattach your spray-skirt and pump the water from your kayak.

1 FACE-UP ASSISTED From a position between the two kayaks, which face in opposite directions, the swimmer lies back, throws an arm over each kayak and hooks one leg into the cockpit.

2 Keep your head back and swing the other leg up into the cockpit. The rescuer provides a lot of stability by leaning across your kayak.

3 Continue sliding into the cockpit. Make sure that you have your sprayskirt fastened, your paddle in hand and that you are stabilized before separating and carrying on.

Solid Foam Float Outrigger

For the solo paddler who is unable to roll, a capsize means a swim. Getting out of the water and back into the kayak quickly without tipping over again is crucial in cold water. If you use a solid foam paddle float, the time-consuming step of inflating the paddle float is eliminated, and it also provides a very stable outrigger.

A sling is a length of webbing or rope that forms a loop that is used to assist a paddler in getting back into her kayak from the water. The loop, used in conjunction with a paddle float, acts as a step up that can be attached to either the cockpit or the paddle shaft.

1 PADDLE FLOAT WITH RESCUE SLING
With the paddle float secured to one blade, slip the sling over the other blade. Place the paddle across the back deck of the kayak with the sling hanging down into the water on the side farthest from you.

2 Reach under the kayak to grab the sling. (It helps to push the kayak away from you without letting go.) Wrap the sling around the paddle shaft on your side.

3 Put the loop under the ball of your foot. Using the sling as you would a stirrup on a horse, hoist yourself up and across the cockpit, keeping your weight on the outrigger side.

Assisted Rescues and Recoveries

It is good practice to always assume that you are going to have to rescue yourself. However, there are times when assistance can be very helpful, especially in the conditions that likely caused the capsize in the first place. When you are put in the position of being a rescuer, the first decision you have to make is, do I get the paddler out of the water and back into a swamped kayak, or can I get the kayak emptied first and then get the paddler back in? The second scenario is nearly always preferable because a swamped kayak is awkward to stay upright in, and it is a time-consuming, physically demanding exercise to pump out a cockpit full of water.

When would you decide it was necessary to get a paddler back into a swamped kayak? Three obvious instances are if the swimmer is not dressed for immersion in cold water, if the swimmer does not have the physical ability to get back into the emptied kayak, or if the swimmer is injured or unconscious. We have demonstrated some of these assisted reentries to give you an idea of the variety available, depending on the conditions. Practice them in wind and waves and you will be prepared when you really need them.

1 ASSISTED RESCUE WITH SLING The rescuer holds the kayaks together and puts the sling around the swimmer's cockpit. The swimmer must step into the rescue sling with the ball of her foot in order to avoid rope entanglement.

2 The rescuer stabilizes the swimmer's kayak while she uses the stirrup to give her a boost up onto the back of the cockpit.

3 The swimmer slips her foot free of the loop and swings her legs into the cockpit while the rescuer stabilizes the kayak.

1 BOW RESCUE The capsized paddler lets the rescuer know that she needs assistance by reaching above the water, with a hand on either side of the hull, slapping the kayak and then sweeping her hands along it to provide a target area.

2 The rescuer approaches the overturned kayak swiftly but carefully. The rescuer has to place his bow within this target area without hurting the person's hands or smashing into the kayak. (You may want to review Stopping in Chapter 8.)

3 The capsized paddler takes hold of the bow with two hands. Try not to exert much pressure on the rescuer's kayak as you simultaneously lift up the underwater knee (knee lift) and press your opposite buttock into your seat (hip snap).

4 Keep your head down until the kayak is upright underneath you.

Practicing the Hip Snap and Knee Lift

This one action will improve your bracing, help in some recoveries and is absolutely essential for a successful roll. To practice it, start with something stationary that provides support for your upper body such as a low dock, the edge of a pool or the bow of someone's kayak.

Your upper and lower body work independently but cooperatively. (Timing is important!) Your hands stay in front of your shoulders, which means you have to rotate your torso to maintain the Paddler's Box position. Rotate toward the support and place both hands on it. Lift your outside knee to pull the kayak upside down on top of you. Your head remains above water. Lay your cheek on your hands. Relax your hips and feel the cockpit rim pressing on your far side. Now, to bring it back up, use the hip snap. This entails pulling up your lower knee and rolling your hips until you feel the cockpit pressing into your other side. Repeat on each side until you feel comfortable. Now try a bow rescue.

Bow Rescue

You can avoid time-consuming swimming and kayak reentries by using the bow rescue. This useful capsize recovery requires some help from a fellow paddler who knows how to respond to your signal for assistance. The capsized paddler slaps the hull and then slides her hands back and forth to give the rescuer a place to aim his bow. The bow is carefully placed within reach of the upside-down kayaker's hands, and she can then hip-snap off of the bow of the other kayak.

1 PADDLE SHAFT RESCUE The capsized paddler signals by raising both hands above the water, slapping the hull and sweeping back and forth along either side. The rescuer approaches the overturned kayak swiftly.

2 Running parallel with the capsized kayak, the rescuer slides his paddle across the overturned kayak, bridging it with his own.

3 The rescuer grabs the nearest hand of the overturned paddler and places it on the paddle shaft.

The Paddle Shaft Rescue

This rescue works like the bow rescue in that the capsized paddler does not wet exit. It requires a certain determination on the part of the capsized paddler to remain upside down and wait for assistance. The rescuer paddles quickly in alongside the capsized kayak, placing his paddle shaft across his kayak and the upside-down hull. The rescuer assists the capsized paddler by placing her hands on the paddle shaft. The capsized paddler uses this support to upright her kayak.

4 The capsized paddler places both hands on the paddle shaft.

5 Pull up on the underwater knee (knee lift) and press the opposite buttock into the seat (hip snap). This is the righting action that brings the kayak to an upright position again.

T-Recovery

The T-Recovery is the fastest way to empty out a swamped cockpit before the swimmer gets back in. (It is assumed that the capsized kayak has sealed bulkheads. Any water running through the cockpit will hit the stern bulkhead and drain out during the T-recovery.) Performing a T-recovery with a heavily loaded kayak can be difficult and requires more strength from the rescuer. The rescuer grabs the bow and pivots his own kayak until it is roughly perpendicular to the overturned kayak, resulting in a T formation. The swimmer assists by moving quickly to the stern end of her kayak. Once the rescuer has hold of the bow of the swamped kayak, the swimmer presses down on the stern to break the vacuum as the cockpit clears the surface. The rescuer lifts the bow, draining water from the cockpit. Roll the kayak upright being careful not to hit the swimmer with the rudder if there is one. The rescuer pivots his kayak so that the two kayaks are parallel, each facing in the opposite direction. In this way, the rescuer can easily lean over the other kayak, creating a very stable raft without getting in the way of the reentering paddler. Secure the paddles so that they do not float away during the reentry. Ensure that the person who capsized has fully recovered with sprayskirt in place and paddle in hand before pushing away from one another.

1 **T-RECOVERY** The rescuer approaches the overturned kayak's bow. The swimmer holds on to her paddle between her legs to free up her hands. The swimmer assists by getting to the stern of the overturned kayak.

2 The swimmer pushes down on the stern to help break the seal created between the cockpit and the surface of the water. The rescuer picks up the bow.

3 With sealed bulkheads, the water drains from the cockpit quickly.

4 The rescuer rolls the kayak back upright, being careful not to hit the swimmer with the rudder if there is one.

5 The rescuer slides the kayak back into the water.

6 The rescuer pivots around the bow, bringing the swimmer's kayak parallel to his but facing in the opposite direction. This capsize recovery is completed using the Side by Side method shown on the next page.

OPPOSITE If you want a child to love kayaking, be one yourself. Avoid long days of paddling from place to place. Summer is a time for sand, sun and swimming.

1 **SIDE BY SIDE** The rescuer comes alongside the overturned kayaker so that the two kayaks are bow to stern.

2 The rescuer assists the swimmer in uprighting the kayak.

3 The rescuer stabilizes the kayak by leaning across it. The swimmer does a scissor kick onto the stern deck and hangs on to the rescuer's hull.

4 Stay low, facing the stern and keeping a firm hold on both kayaks. The rescuer can guide your legs into the cockpit.

5 Twist and drop down into the seat.

6 The rescuer stabilizes the two kayaks while the rescued paddler empties her cockpit. This sprayskirt has a waterproof zipper opening that allows the sprayskirt to be fastened around the coaming while pumping out.

All-In

All-in means everyone has capsized and wet exited. If the conditions are rough and the paddlers are inexperienced, this scenario has the potential to escalate into a disaster. Yet with a bit of practice, the situation can be handled fairly quickly and efficiently as the capsized paddlers help one another get back into their kayaks, pumped out and stabilized. Paddlers have to be traveling in close proximity to one another for this kind of rescue to work.

1 **ALL-IN** Bring the kayaks alongside one another, in the bow-to-stern formation. One paddler is holding the paddle between her legs and holding both kayaks together. The other paddler swims up onto the two overturned hulls, reaching for the cockpit of the farthest kayak.

2 He pulls the outside kayak toward him, uprighting it. He continues to lie across the overturned kayak, stabilizing the upright one ready for the swimmer in the water to now reenter. He holds both paddles between the kayaks.

1 **TANDEM ALL-IN PADDLE FLOAT RECOVERY** Instead of simply turning the kayak upright, try lifting it from the cockpits together on a count of three. This way, some of the water will drain out.

2 The stern person gets in first. This can be done as a scramble without aid or a paddle float can be used to provide more stability as shown here.

PAGE 135 As an enormous iceberg floats by, only one-tenth of it visible above the surface, chunks of it frequently break off, changing its equilibrium. When that occurs, there is a tremendous explosion, the iceberg rocks and tilts, and then quietly settles as if nothing ever happened.

3 Keeping a low, reasonably horizontal profile, she swims up onto the stern deck and slides her legs into the cockpit.

4 The now upright paddler assists the swimmer in righting the other kayak. She is responsible for tucking the paddles under the deck rigging so they won't float away.

5 Two kayaks rafted together like this with one paddler draped over the other kayak creates a very stable position for both paddlers. The swimmer scissor-kicks onto the back deck, and slides into the cockpit. With sprayskirts partially fastened, the two paddlers stabilize each other's kayaks while pumping out their flooded cockpits.

3 The first swimmer is using a paddle float recovery to reenter while the other swimmer stabilizes the kayak.

4 The second swimmer reenters using a technique similar to the scramble. Twisting to face the outrigger and keeping his weight over the paddle float side of the kayak, he slides his legs and bottom into the cockpit. The other paddler maintains stability with the paddle float.

5 With both kayakers aboard, they can now pump out one at a time while the other one stabilizes the kayak.

Hand of God

Having to use the Hand of God gets even a very experienced paddler's adrenalin flowing as it involves a serious situation of injury, entrapment or unconsciousness. The victim's kayak is upside down and he has not wet exited nor raised his hands above the surface requesting a bow or paddle shaft rescue. The rescuer has to be close by and work very swiftly to get the victim's head above water. Pull up beside the capsized kayak, reach over the overturned hull and grab the victim's PFD or any good handhold. To right the victim, apply downward pressure on the upper edge of their kayak while pulling the victim up by the shoulder or PFD strap.

1 HAND OF GOD The capsized paddler is unconscious or for some reason cannot get out of the kayak. The rescuer moves swiftly alongside the overturned kayak and reaches across it.

Scoop Rescue for Injured or Unconscious Paddler

If a paddler has capsized, wet exited and is injured with, for instance, a shoulder dislocation, a fellow paddler can help him reenter his kayak using the scoop rescue. The rescuer comes in parallel to the victim's kayak. The rescuer turns the kayak on its side, partially submerging the cockpit so that the swimmer can be floated in and positioned over the seat. If the victim is conscious, he can assist the rescuer by lying back or leaning forward to lower his center of gravity. This makes it easier for the rescuer to pull the boat upright using the same technique as with the Hand of God. In the water, a small person is not at as big a disadvantage in assisting a larger person as they are on land.

2 The rescuer grabs hold of the cockpit rim or the victim's PFD, pulling the kayak and victim upright. Continuing to hold on to the victim, the rescuer must simultaneously push down on the high side of the kayak to roll the kayak under the victim and bring him into an upright position.

3 At this point, you have the whole situation to assess, especially if you do have an unconscious paddler. Can you administer first aid and revive the victim? Can you get to shore? Is there anyone else there with you?

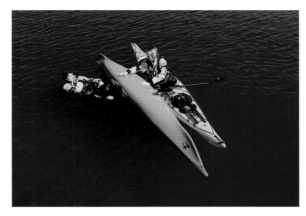  

1 **SCOOP** First the rescuer must get the kayak partway turned over with the cockpit partially submerged.

2 Keep the gunwale close to the water to make it easier to float the victim in. Grab hold of the injured paddler's PFD.

3 Stuff, push, float — do whatever it takes — to assist the injured paddler in getting his legs into the cockpit.

4 With a firm hold on the injured paddler's PFD, apply all your weight to the high edge of his kayak and push down. This will roll the kayak beneath him, which will be much more successful than attempting to actually lift the victim in.

5 Continue to push down on the victim's kayak and simultaneously pull the victim toward you, keeping him low.

6 Once upright, the victim's sprayskirt needs to be put on and the cockpit pumped out. See Chapter 9 for ways to stabilize an injured or helpless person in a kayak for towing.

Kayakers who travel this line between the land and the water can't help but be awed by the gray fists of granite that protrude into a lake shaped by glaciers ten millennia ago.

TX Recovery and On-Water Kayak Repair

This recovery has a couple of uses. The first one is to empty a kayak that has flotation instead of sealed bulkheads. This comes with a caution. A kayak full of water is extremely heavy. It is possible to gouge, scrape or crack the kayaks in this process. Carefully drag the swimmer's kayak across your cockpit until the kayaks form an X. The swimmer can stabilize the rescuer's kayak at the bow. Make sure the rescuer's sprayskirt is firmly fixed around the cockpit coaming before the kayak is overturned and emptied. Overturn the kayak and rock in a see-saw motion to drain water from both ends of the kayak before it is flipped upright and returned to the water.

The other use for a TX recovery is to examine and or perform an on-water hull repair when you are unable to get to shore. First, empty the water out using the T-recovery then pull the damaged kayak across your coaming. Roll the cockpit toward you while the swimmer stabilizes your kayak. The swimmer can help stabilize and inspect the hull with the rescuer. If the damage is a puncture or crack causing the kayak to leak, apply a temporary patch of plumber's tape, which will adhere to a damp surface. The simplest field repairs are done with duct tape but it does not stick to a wet surface. Shoe Goo, two-part epoxy or a marine sealant can be used to make a better repair once you get to shore. Even though field repairs are often done under duress and in hurried conditions, you should attempt to do the best looking job that you can, since sealants such as two-part epoxy are difficult to remove later on.

1 **TX RECOVERY** The rescuer empties the kayak that needs repair then pulls it up onto his deck. The swimmer can stabilize the rescuer's kayak by wrapping her arms and legs around it at the bow.

2 The rescuer rolls the kayak over by pulling the cockpit toward himself until it is fully overturned and balancing across his kayak.

3 The swimmer can straddle the bow deck to assist in the inspection for damage to the hull.

4 From here, if it is calm, the hull can be dried and repaired.

Towing

Experienced paddlers always have towing options and know how to use them and the equipment associated with them. Towing can mean transporting a swimmer to the safety of shore or back to his kayak. Not all tows have to do with rescuing someone. In fact, more often than not, a tow is used to give a tired paddler a bit of extra power, or as a safety precaution in crossing an open stretch of water. A tow can assist a seasick or injured paddler. We have demonstrated just a few methods here but there are many others. Some involve rope; others don't. (Keep in mind that the conditions that made the tow necessary can also create potentially dangerous situations where people get tangled in the rope.)

The most basic assistance doesn't involve any rope. In a close-contact tow, the rescuer and paddler in need of rescue are in contact with one another throughout the tow. One effective method for moving a kayaker quickly doesn't involve any equipment at all. The rescuer simply paddles up to the kayaker in need and allows him to lean on the rescuer's kayak for stability and then paddles on. The kayak being assisted can be facing either way in relation to the rescuer so that the rescuer may have this person leaning on the bow or stern of their kayak. It is a great way to move someone a short distance quickly, perhaps to help someone who has lost his paddle to get clear of the surf zone.

If a swimmer has inadvertently gotten separated from his kayak, a rescuer can assist by transporting the swimmer onto the bow or stern of the rescuer's kayak. Hugging the bow works fine for short distances, but piggy-backing the stern of the rescue kayak works better for somewhat longer distances. The rescuer instructs the swimmer to press him or herself flat to lower their center of gravity as much as possible and create a more stable situation for the rescuer. The piggy-back technique is very useful when you need to get a swimmer out of cold water. Meanwhile another kayaker can be dealing with the swamped kayak to get it emptied and then assist with getting the kayaker back in.

CLOSE-CONTACT TOW This is a close-contact tow because the person needing assistance is in close contact with the assisting kayak, leaning into either the stern or bow of the rescuer's kayak, depending on which direction the rescuer comes from. The beauty of this tow is the speed with which it can be employed. In surf, for instance, the rescuer can quickly paddle up to someone who has lost his paddle. The rescuer has only to come in parallel, and barely needs to slow down.

1 **PIGTAIL TOW** Using a pigtail tow, the kayak (being towed) rides far enough back not to interfere with the paddler's strokes.

2 A line as short as 3 feet (1 m) can be used for a close-contact tow for a wayward kayak or to keep an injured paddler close at hand for a short-distance tow.

TOWING A KAYAK If a swimmer lets go of his kayak in a capsize, the wind can quickly sweep it away, requiring another paddler to pursue it. A pigtail tow rope with a built-in extension line comes in handy for retrieving it.

Swimmer on Deck

If a swimmer becomes separated from his kayak, then the two have to be rescued and brought back together. If there are several people available, someone in the group can catch the kayak and tow it back. The swimmer may need to be moved. If the water is cold, the swimmer can lie face down on the back deck of the rescuer's kayak. If you need to move someone quickly for a short distance, and there isn't time for the person to get out of the water, paddle quickly toward him and he can latch on to the bow of your kayak, with arms and legs hugging it.

1 TOWING: SWIMMER ON DECK This technique, in which the swimmer grabs on to the bow in this position, is useful when you want to move someone to safety quickly over a short distance, such as in the surf zone.

2 This technique is most useful when you need to get a swimmer out of cold water, or moved quickly. The swimmer slides up onto the back deck of the kayak, lying flat to keep his center of gravity as low as possible.

USE OF PADDLE FLOATS IN TOWING Paddle floats can be used to stabilize a sick or injured paddler who is being towed. Attach a paddle float to each of the blades then fasten the paddle shaft to the kayak to ensure it is anchored in a perpendicular position.

1 All clear. Come ahead.

2 Stop. Stay where you are.

3 Point the paddle blade in the direction you want those following you to go. (Never point at an obstacle; point only toward a safe route.)

Signals

Before heading out on the water with a friend or group, make sure everyone knows the universally accepted paddle and hand signals to communicate. On a windy day it is especially difficult to make your voice heard. Every paddler should wear a PDF and each PDF should have a pea-less whistle attached to it. It is an easy way to attract attention with one blast; in an emergency, use three blasts.

The paddle signals are shown here. These can be done with your arms but the paddle shows up better from the low vantage point of a kayaker. These signals are especially useful to guide paddlers to shore while landing in surf, when the signaler is already on the shore.

4 A vertical paddle waved back and forth indicates an emergency.

CHAPTER 11

NAVIGATION

MASTER THE SKILLS OF NAVIGATION and you can know where you are, where you have come from and where you are going. When choosing the best route to travel, you will consider many factors, including the scenery, wind, weather and time of day, the skill and well-being of the paddlers, the tides, and avoidance of natural and manmade dangers. Yet navigating a kayak is an art as well as a skill and it takes a greater sense of the whole than just reading the map, the compass or a GPS (global positioning system) can provide. When you travel by kayak, you move at a natural speed. You experience changes of landscape at a pace that enables you to be very observant. Your senses have time to capture the essence of every place in a way that no motorized form of travel can.

Some people have a knack for perceiving the whole faster than others. For most of us, it comes with an accumulation of real-life experience. You can see it in sport, art, music, photography, math and writing. It takes experience to navigate a kayak. Knowing how fast you are traveling, being aware of changes in current or wind direction, estimating the time of day by where the light falls, and noting and remembering natural markers such as the shape of a headland or the changing color of the water as you pass a river mouth — these are the kinds of things a perceptive and observant paddler learns by experience.

Familiar places on a bright, clear day quickly become foreign lands if you are unable to find your way in fog without your sense of sight. Navigation is partly the art of learning to use a map and compass, but it is also learning to be observant of your surroundings in changing conditions.

Nautical Talk

The following terms come up frequently in this chapter. In order to simplify the explanations, we have defined them here.

AIDS FOR NAVIGATION These aids include buoys, beacons, fog signals, light signals and radio beacons. They are listed on marine charts and updated by the Coast Guard on a regular basis.

BEARING A compass direction to a landmark, a navigation aid or some identified stationary point of reference.

BACK BEARING The compass direction opposite to the bearing. To calculate it, either add or subtract 180 degrees to the bearing.

COMPASS ROSE The symbol on the nautical chart that shows both magnetic and true north bearings.

COURSE The direction in which you travel as a result of all forces.

DEAD RECKONING TRACK The line you are paddling presumed correct given the factors of time elapsed, paddling speed and the direction in which you are traveling. (It is used at night or in the fog when you cannot see any landmarks).

DECLINATION The variation between true north (geographic) and magnetic north (where the compass points). Declination is noted in the center of the compass rose.

ESTIMATED POSITION When you adjust a dead reckoning position based on a belief about the effect of wind or current on your position, you have your estimated position.

FIX The intersection of two or more lines of position (LOPs).

HEADING This is the direction in which the kayak is pointed.

KNOT This measurement of speed equals 1 nautical mile per hour.

LATITUDE These imaginary lines run parallel to the equator.

LINE OF POSITION (LOP) A range used to determine your position relative to a charted object.

LONGITUDE On a map, these imaginary lines are the meridians that encircle the globe passing through the north and south poles with Greenwich, England, representing 0 degrees.

NAUTICAL MILE A distance of 1.15 statute miles or 1.87 kilometers. One minute of latitude equals 1 nautical mile.

RANGE An imaginary straight line created when you align two objects, natural or manmade.

SCALE OF MAPS A small scale means smaller details over a larger area, so you can see more of the landscape but in less detail. Large scale means larger detail over a smaller area, which is what you want for kayaking.

SOUNDINGS The depth of the water in feet or fathoms (1 fathom equals 6 feet or about 2 meters).

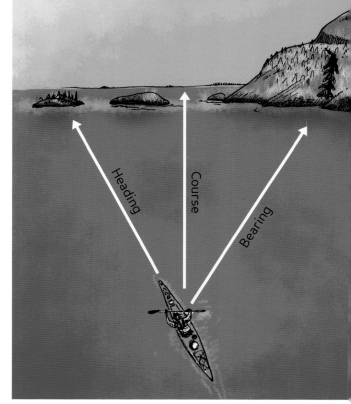

Differences Between a Heading, Course and Bearing

Your **HEADING** is the direction in which your kayak is pointed; your **COURSE** is the direction in which you travel as a result of all forces; and your **BEARING** is the direction in which your compass points from you to a particular location.

Navigational Tools

COMPASS A deck-mounted compass is easiest to use while paddling; however, you should also carry a pocket compass. Check the accuracy of your deck compass before getting underway. Magnetic deviation can occur if anything containing iron is nearby. With a handheld compass, you can be seated in the kayak and take bearings to points other than the direction in which your kayak is headed. Use it to take bearings while you are ashore, or for any on-land travel. A compass can be used in conjunction with a map and a watch to inform you of your direction of travel and to help you figure out how fast you are traveling. By using back bearings and cross bearings, paddlers can determine their position, recognize landmarks on the map, and estimate the effect of wind and or current by comparing the intended course with the actual direction of traveled. A compass will help you notice a change in wind or current direction.

An electronic **GPS** (global positioning system) receiver can accurately pinpoint your location. It can also give you measurements of speed and distance. Before setting out on your journey, you can log in way points, locations such as open water crossings, campsites and take-out points, for instance. The GPS is an amazing tool but, as an electronic, battery-operated device, it is subject to failure. First and foremost, the knowledge of navigation needs be in your head and you need to have and to know how to use a map and a compass.

The Small Craft **NAV-AID,** developed by Charles Sutherland, is a simple device that is handy to use on the water. The small plastic square has a compass rose with two sets of markings. The outside circle shows magnetic bearings while the inside circle shows the magnetic back bearings. The string, or bearing line, coming up through the center of the circle is used to measure a distance on the map. The edge of the Nav-Aid can be used to draw straight lines between points on the map case with your china marker. Depending on the type of map you are using, you can add nautical mile, kilometer or statute mile marks along the bearing line.

A **COURSE PLOTTER** is a sheet of acetate with parallel lines marked on it. Overlay it on your map, lining it up with the magnetic reading on your chart's compass rose. It is a useful tool for measuring distances and directions between points while underway.

DIVIDERS and **PARALLEL RULERS** are pre-trip planning tools used on a map to chart out a route measuring distances and directions between points.

Keep your charts and maps in a waterproof, transparent chart case while traveling. Chart cases made for paddlers have hooks for attachment to the kayak deck rigging. They will lie flat on the deck of the kayak so you can read them while you are paddling. A roll Velcro closure is secure yet easy to open. On a longer trip that requires multiple maps, you will constantly be bringing out the maps, reviewing and refolding them while on shore. Anticipating the journey to come is both a source of enjoyment and a constant on-going exercise in planning for all eventualities in the days ahead.

Topographic Maps and Nautical Charts

A kayaker travels the border between land and sea, so topographic maps and nautical charts are both useful. A kayaker dealing with tides or marine traffic on the sea coast depends on a nautical chart. Kayakers navigating the shoreline of an inland lake rely more on the topographic features of hills and valleys to know where they are. Learn how to read information from both sources.

TOPOGRAPHIC MAPS (below, left) describe the land with its contours and physical geographic features such as rivers, mountains, hills and wetlands. Manmade features such as roads and railways are marked. These maps also give true and magnetic north as well as declination. The line of 0 degrees declination runs from the true North Pole south through Florida. Unless you are on this 0 degree line, the north on your map is not the north your compass is pointing to until you adjust for declination.

A NAUTICAL CHART (below, right) shows on-water features including depths, description of the bottom and near-shore landscape details such as shoals, rocks and islands. At the center of the compass rose you will find the variation between true and magnetic north. Since we follow our magnetic compass on the deck of our kayak, the inner circle, or magnetic compass bearing, is the one to use. A chart also includes the man-made aids for navigation such as buoys, beacons, lights and harbors. If you are depending on a nautical chart's navigation markers, beacons and buoys, get the most up-to-date one available.

All your pre-trip route planning may seem obsolete once you are underway as conditions and priorities change. However, the more you pore over the maps before a trip, the more familiar the route becomes, and the more information you have to draw upon while making quick decisions in fast-changing wind, weather or emergencies. Keep your maps and charts in a waterproof transparent map case. Use a china marker to write on your chart case or even the deck of your kayak. It is easy to remove and will enable you to keep track of information about your course.

The chart scale most useful for a kayaker is 1:40,000 (1.5 inches equals 1 statute mile). The comparable topographic map scale is 1:50,000. This scale means that 1.25 inches equals a mile or 2 centimeters equals a kilometer, giving you sufficient detail for the speed at which a kayaker travels. On journeys of two weeks or more in length, Gary and I carry a smaller scale map as well as the more detailed maps, as they provide a better overview for long-term planning. National, provincial and state parks sometimes have fairly accurate overview maps on which you will be able to see your entire trip. All charts and maps have a name, number, the scale, longitude and latitude lines, and an edition date.

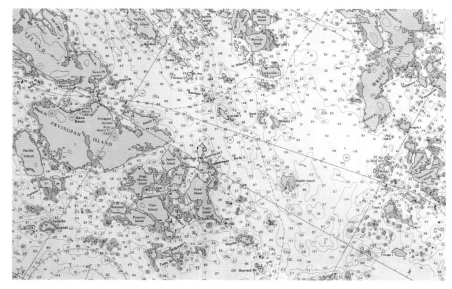

Latitude and Longitude

Looking at a globe, the imaginary lines of longitude are the ones that run through the North and South poles; the prime meridian of 0 degrees longitude runs through Greenwich, England. The imaginary lines of latitude run around the globe parallel to the equator, the equator being the biggest circle at 0 degrees latitude. The latitude scale can be used as a measurement of distance. One degree of latitude is 60 nautical miles; 1 minute of latitude is 1 nautical mile. The longitude and latitude coordinates on your maps and on the GPS receiver can help you pinpoint exact locations.

In a practical sense, this information is most useful in providing an exact description of your location in the event of an emergency when radioing for assistance. Landmarks, compass directions and navigation aids are what the traveling kayaker uses to navigate the majority of the time. With the advent of GPS receivers and satellite mapping images, wilderness travelers sometimes get wrapped up in the technology, forgetting the practicality of observing their surroundings. Your attention should be on the landscape around you so you are at all times aware of the total picture: where you have come from and where you are going, as well as the changing conditions and how they can affect you.

How to Figure Out Where You Are

There are any number of mathematical equations for figuring out how far you are from shore, how fast you are moving, where a vessel is going to pass

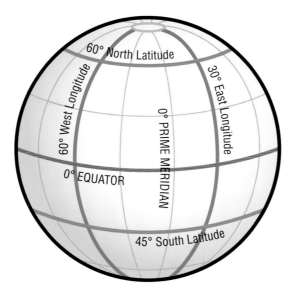

in relation to you, and how to figure out where you are when you get disoriented or moved about by wind and tides. But we have limited our review to a few simple practical tips, as there are whole books devoted to the art of navigation. Apart from keen observation skills, what you most need to know as a sea kayaker is how to read a topographic map and a nautical chart, and how to use a compass. When you start out from a known point, you need to make sure you know where this point is on your map and that you are sure of the direction that you are taking from this known point. If you are using a GPS receiver, be sure to back this information up by following a map as well.

Learn how to read a compass bearing. If you can see where you want to go from where you are, point your kayak in that direction and read the magnetic heading on your compass (a deck-mounted compass being the most useful

for a kayaker). Note the heading and follow this course. If you want to take a bearing from your chart or topographic map, see page 155.

> **NAVIGATION TIP LOOKING BACK**
> Look behind you often to get a sense of what the landscape looks like in the opposite direction. Not looking back from where you have come is a very common mistake wilderness travelers make, whether on land or on the water.

Dead Reckoning

In the absence of a GPS receiver, dead reckoning is used to determine your position by keeping track of previously known positions using your speed of travel, and the amount of time and the direction in which you have been traveling. In a thick fog or on a dark night, you can figure out, with reasonable accuracy over the course of an hour's paddling, where you are if you know these three things. The longer you travel on this path, the greater the margin for error grows, especially as dead reckoning does not take into account the effect that any current and drift are having upon you. Careful observations of these can be factored into the equation to give you an estimated position. However, even this cannot account for the fact it is impossible for anyone to paddle a dead-straight line from point to point without the aid of an on-board electronic navigational device (such as a GPS) or constant opportunities to confirm your position with sightings of recognizable land features or navigational aids.

Setting a Dead Reckoning Track and Aiming Off

It is spring and the fog, thick as a cloud, has settled over Georgian Bay. There are many islands and, even in clear conditions, navigating can be a challenge. You want to make a crossing between Fryingpan Island and Wreck Island, which you are unable to see. Mark on your chart the line between where you are on the south end of Fryingpan Island and where you want to go on the tip of Wreck Island. Using your Nav-Aid (see page 155), you determine that this line is 1.75 miles (1.5 nautical miles) in length. Now using the inner ring of the compass rose (the magnetic north compass reading that a kayaker follows) you note a south-southeast course of 150 degrees. Orient your kayak until your deck compass reads 150 degrees. If you travel at a speed of 2.5 knots and follow this exact heading, providing no other variables enter the picture, you will end up on the tip of Wreck Island in 37 minutes. Without confirming your position along the way with a GPS or a visual aid, you are on a dead reckoning track.

In real paddling conditions when you cannot confirm your position by visual or electronic aid, there is always a margin of error growing greater the further you travel. It is better to aim off, which means that you will deliberately miss your target to one side or the other. This is an especially useful technique to employ while crossing a channel in low visibility, especially when wind or current may affect your dead reckoning track. When you are just not sure where your landfall will be, you want to make sure that you end up hitting the far shore certain that you are one side of your target or the other. If you deliberately aim off, you will know which way to turn to paddle to your intended destination.

Reviewing the map, we can see that halfway to Wreck Island there is a small group of islands. Instead of traveling on a bearing of 150 degrees (the dead reckoning track), deliberately follow a compass bearing of 145 degrees instead. Traveling at 2.5 knots, you should arrive at these islands within 15 minutes. (You can then use them as confirmation of your position along your route.) Continue on this bearing of 145 degrees to the shore of Wreck Island. In this ghost-white world, you may not know exactly where you have landed on Wreck Island but you will know that when you hit shore, you must turn right or southwest in order to reach the tip of Wreck Island.

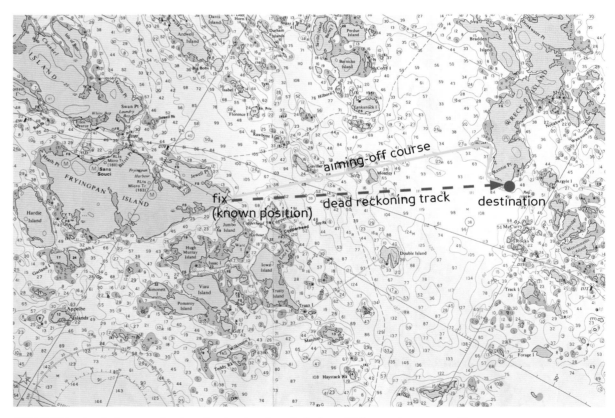

ABOVE This chart shows a dead reckoning track and aiming off from a known position.

OPPOSITE When you are traveling in the Arctic your sense of perspective changes without the familiar scale of trees. What looks like a ten-minute paddle can easily be more than an hour away.

Ranges

You can use your compass to follow a straight path on the water, but there is a more practical and accurate way if the weather is fair and clear. Look ahead on the course you are following. Find two or more distant objects aligned along this path. They might be a crooked white pine on the hill with flaming red maple tree in the foreground near shore, or a flagpole, a boathouse and a cottage in the distance. If you stay on course, your two (or three) ranges will remain in line. You will quickly notice if you get off this line of position. If the pine tree moves to the left of the red maple tree, then you have drifted left of your course. Just paddle back to the right until they are aligned again. If the cottage and boathouse are drifting to the right of the flagpole, you are right of your intended path. Just paddle to port (your left) to get back on line. As your course changes as you travel along, just make note of new ranges and travel accordingly. Be cautious of following manmade navigation ranges in busy harbor areas, as you could easily

Drifted left of the range   Lining up the beaver lodge, spruce and white pine creates a range to paddle in a straight line.   Drifted right of the range

find yourself in the path of marine traffic much bigger than you.

My father-in-law used to use ranges all the time when we were out fishing. He would line up two ranges, or aligned landmarks, in one direction and two ranges in another direction and then he would know exactly where he was in relation to a particular favorite fishing spot. This technique combined with his knowledge of the underwater landscape learned over time was much more impressive than using a fish-finder.

Like my father-in-law, we use this technique making note of landmarks and cross-referencing them visually and mentally with landmarks that are 90 degrees to the direction in which we are traveling. In this way, we are able to keep an eye on our progress without having to keep stopping to write things down.

line of sight

Line of Position

If you are not sure where you are, or you just want to mark a spot on the water, you can use a compass bearing to figure out a line of position. Take a bearing on a charted feature, natural or manmade, then draw the back bearing (just add or subtract 180 degrees to the bearing) beginning at the feature. You are somewhere along that line. In order to know exactly where you are on the line, take another bearing in a different direction and draw the back bearing, in other words, another line of position. You are where the two lines intersect. You now have a fix on your position.

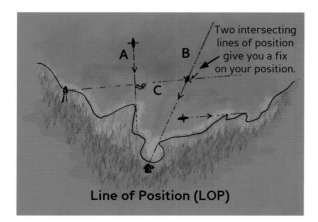

Two intersecting lines of position give you a fix on your position.

Line of Position (LOP)

Rules of the Road

Although technically a kayaker has the right of way because a kayak is a self-propelled vessel, that kind of thinking is like the pedestrian who steps in front of a truck and says he has the right of way. It doesn't matter if the kayaker is right if he gets run over by a ferry boat. Always paddle defensively and yield to motorized vessels despite what the law says about who has the right of way. Yachts and large vessels are required to have running lights and you should know the light requirements of different vessels if you travel at night in areas of boat traffic. At night, a kayaker can tell which way the vessel is moving by the color of these lights. As paddlers, we are required to have a white light aboard from sunset to sunrise.

LEFT These lines of position are ranges used to determine your position relative to charted objects such as **A**, two points of land; **B**, a point of land and a building; and **C**, a marker buoy and a communication tower.

Are You On a Collision Course?

If a motorized vessel is headed your way and you are not sure whether its path will pass behind, in front or collide with you, a quick method to check this is to look at the angle between your bow and the other vessel. Hold out a straight arm or paddle to give yourself a line to look down. Note the angle: if it increases over time, you are going to pass in front of the vessel; if it decreases, you are going to pass behind it; and if the angle stays the same, watch out because you are on a collision course. You can also take a compass bearing on the vessel heading your way and monitor the bearing closely as you keep paddling.

At night, the lights will tell a story, too. An unchanging green and red light means you are on a collision course, a red light means you are looking at the vessel's port side passing by, while green is its starboard side. If the light is white, the vessel is traveling away from you.

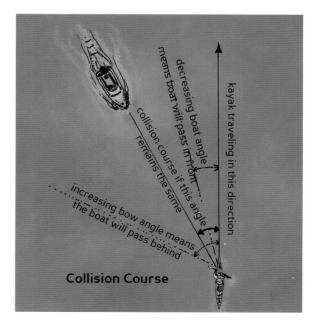

decreasing boat angle means boat will pass in front

collision course if this angle remains the same

increasing bow angle means the boat will pass behind

kayak traveling in this direction

Collision Course

Estimating Distances

It helps to have a sense of what things look like from specific distances. When I was growing up, there was a small lighthouse one of the cottagers had set upon a shoal in the middle of the bay. All summer long my sister, brother and I would paddle or swim over to the lighthouse. From our shore I could clearly see the grain of wood and the metal rings. This 100-yard distance became my mental measuring stick, one that I still use when estimating a distance. Likewise you can practice this with people on shore or plants that are common to your region. Notice how far away you are when you can distinguish people from little blobs, then see a body with legs and arms and finally are close enough to recognize a face.

Calculating Bearings

As a navigator in your kayak, one of the most important things you need to be able to do apart from being observant of your surroundings is calculate your bearings. There are two approaches.

CALCULATE A BEARING FROM A TOPOGRAPHIC MAP Find north on your handheld compass and then orient the map so that it is facing north. Find your start and end points for the section of the route you wish to take a bearing for. Place your compass on the map, and align the straight edge of the compass case with the imaginary straight line between the two points. Turn the dial on the compass until the arrow once again aligns with north. Read the magnetic compass direction from the start point to the end point.

CALCULATE A BEARING WHILE IN YOUR KAYAK Point the bow of your kayak at an object while you are traveling and read the deck compass. This is your magnetic bearing. Making sure you are going in the correct general direction sounds like a simple thing, but it is a common enough mistake to read the opposite side of the compass, setting you on a course exactly opposite to your intended direction. Be sure to approximate the direction so that you don't get confused. If you are traveling roughly west then the compass should read somewhere around 270 degrees. If it reads somewhere around 90 degrees, then you are going in the wrong direction. Turn around.

CALCULATE A BACK BEARING If the heading you are on is less than 180 degrees, add 180 degrees. If the heading you are on is more than 180 degrees, subtract 180 degrees. This information is immediately available on your Nav-Aid.

PLOT A COURSE USING A NAV-AID (See photo, left.) Mark a straight line between two points on your course. Place the Nav-Aid's center on the starting point and align its north with the magnetic north on the chart or map. Stretch the Nav-Aid's bearing line along the course to the end point marked on your map. The string will lie across the Nav-Aid's compass rose showing the magnetic course heading you need to take. To determine the true north heading instead, follow the instructions above with the one difference. Place the Nav-Aid's center over your starting point and align the topographic map's or chart's true north with the Nav-Aid's north.

CHAPTER 12

WEATHER, WIND, WAVES AND TIDES

WHEN YOU ARE A PADDLER, you have to be your own weather forecaster. Long ago, when most people were hunters, gatherers or farmers, an awareness of the weather would have been as natural to you as breathing. You would have absorbed whatever was happening around you all the time, remembering past weather to paint your predictions for the future. Today the clouds come and go, the moon waxes and wanes, the night becomes day and, amazingly, these great events go unnoticed except by people who still live in accordance with the weather. As a kayaker, you can once again be on intimate terms with the natural world. Only half of sea kayaking is taking the strokes. The other half is understanding and respecting the environment that embraces your tiny watercraft.

One of the most challenging aspects of any outdoor pursuit is learning how to read the real world around you. You can learn all about your kayak and associated gear. With practice, you can master getting in and out of this narrow craft, and you can learn a repertoire of strokes and maneuvers and capsize recovery and rescue options. But when you understand what the wind is doing to the water, what the topography is doing to affect the wind and waves, what the storm front is likely to do, you are much better prepared to actually go out tripping in your kayak. Paying attention to the elements is a lifelong pursuit.

OPPOSITE Paddling part of Ontario's Great Lakes Heritage Coast on a brisk September day, we glimpse the first hints of crimson and gold among the pines. The snow-white quartz hills of the La Cloche range are a stunning backdrop to this landscape.

RIGHT Catching the wind with a parafoil kite is an enjoyable way to spend an afternoon too windy to paddle.

Clouds

Clouds are beautiful to watch. Who has not laid down on a beach or in the grass and watched their changing shapes? As the earth spins, warm air rises, gathering moisture from oceans, lakes and rivers. Then it cools and condenses into clouds of various shape and color appearing at different altitudes. The area between different cloud masses is where the conditions we experience — the wind and rain — are created. Clouds are the messengers of weather ahead, be it fair or foul; they always tell a story. Wise paddlers will learn how to read them. Study cloud formations and light changes every day everywhere you go. Start noticing whether it is dewy in the morning, or dry. Notice if the air is humid or fresh. The more you understand the natural world around you, the more you respect it; the more you respect it, the more you love it.

Weather Information Sources

Predictions of larger scale weather patterns can be found on the television, internet, radio and newspaper. For the necessary smaller scale forecast more accurate for predicting local conditions, use your VHF radio, weather radio, ask local inhabitants and refer to observations in your personal weather journal.

CLOUD FORMATIONS High wispy clouds of the upper atmosphere known as mare's tails foretell of changing weather within a day or two. Rainbow halos created when the sun and the moon shine through these clouds are a further sign of precipitation ahead.

This rapidly moving air mass is a cold front pushing under a warm air mass and forcing it upward. A dark sky such as this indicates high winds and blinding rain are imminent, a threatening situation for a kayaker on the water.

As warm moist air is driven up by an approaching cold front, a cumulonimbus thunderhead resembling a gigantic anvil forms. Here the plume at the flattened top points in the wind's direction and rain is already falling. Lightning and thunder often accompany these clouds.

Fair-weather cumulous clouds are formed by rising bubbles of warm air. Their flat bases mark the height where the air reaches its dew point and condensation begins.

OPPOSITE Storm over Batchawana Bay.

Predicting the Weather

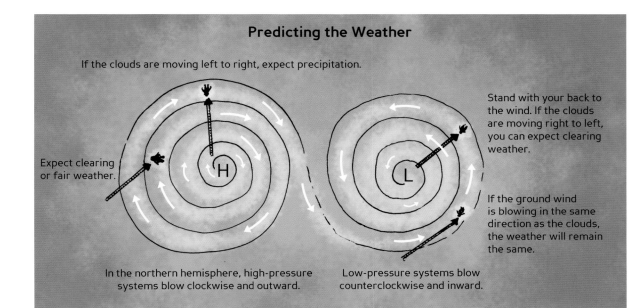

If the clouds are moving left to right, expect precipitation.

Expect clearing or fair weather.

H

In the northern hemisphere, high-pressure systems blow clockwise and outward.

Stand with your back to the wind. If the clouds are moving right to left, you can expect clearing weather.

L

If the ground wind is blowing in the same direction as the clouds, the weather will remain the same.

Low-pressure systems blow counterclockwise and inward.

TIP PREDICTING THE WEATHER

Stand with your back to the wind. If the clouds overhead are moving from your right to your left (in the northern hemisphere), the front has moved through and you can expect drier weather. The wind is said to be veering. If the wind is to your back and the clouds run the same way as the wind, the weather is going to remain the same for a while. If the clouds overhead are moving left to right with the wind coming at your back, you are in for some precipitation, and the wind is said to be backing. In low pressure, the winds are strongest at the center of the low; if you are where that low center is, it is not a good time or place to be paddling.

Warm and Cold Weather Systems

If you have ever watched the weather broadcast on television, you have witnessed the global circulation of air in the earth's upper atmosphere. These weather systems can cover hundreds of miles. On a large scale, the weather is the seasons.

In our temperate climate, these are described as spring, summer, fall and winter. On a kayaker's scale, we are interested in what is happening with weather on a local level, and for a short period of time.

High-Pressure and Low-Pressure Systems

When there is a lot of air pressing down on us from the upper atmosphere, it is described as a high-pressure system. It means fair weather. There are warm and cold high-pressure systems. When air moves from a high-pressure system to a low-pressure system, it travels down what is called a pressure slope. Storm winds are found where there is a great difference in air pressure between the high and low systems and the pressure slope is steep. In the northern hemisphere, high-pressure systems move clockwise, spiraling outward, and low-pressure systems spiral inward, counterclockwise. (The opposite is true south of the equator.) After a storm front goes through, you will notice strong winds that veer in a counterclockwise direction and the weather grows clear and fine. It can be warm or cold.

PRESSURE SYSTEMS Where a difference in air pressure exists in adjoining areas, the air will flow from higher to lower pressure, causing wind. Here a fast-moving cold front brings an abrupt weather change as the cold air pushes into the warm, moist air mass. Paddlers should be aware of the likelihood of a brief, violent downpour from an enormous cumulonimbus thunderhead — and should hurry to find shelter off the water.

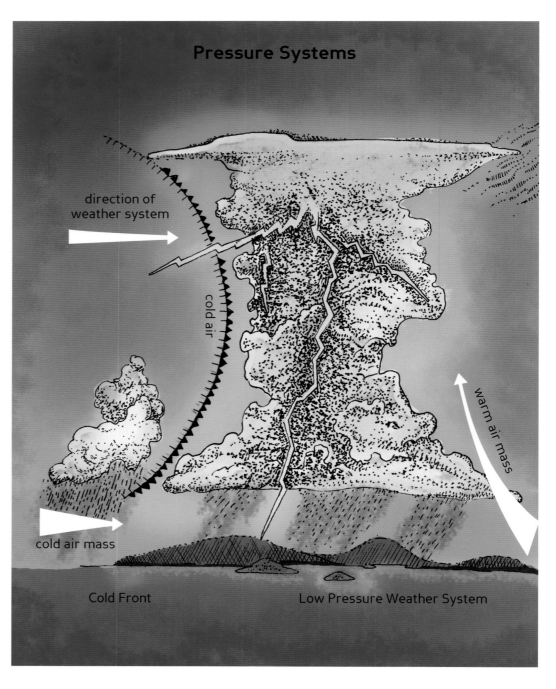

Pressure Systems

direction of weather system

cold air

warm air mass

cold air mass

Cold Front

Low Pressure Weather System

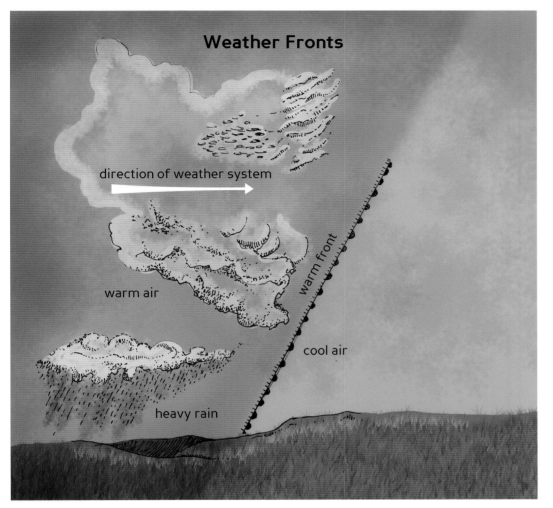

Weather Fronts

direction of weather system

warm air

warm front

cool air

heavy rain

WEATHER FRONTS At our temperate latitude, low-pressure systems bring rain, wind, thunder, lightning and hail. A kayaker needs to learn how to read the signs leading into these conditions. Low-pressure systems in the northern hemisphere flow counterclockwise and inward. High-pressure (fine weather) systems flow clockwise, circling outward from the center.

Warm Fronts and Cold Fronts

Warm and cold fronts are leading edges of two different kinds of low-pressure systems. These fronts separate warm and cold air masses. It is here at the boundaries between warm and cold air that the most dramatic weather effects are felt and seen. Fronts have characteristic cloud and wind patterns. At home, it is a great exercise to monitor the clouds, wind, temperature and barometric pressure every day over a few weeks. You will be able to see patterns and make your own predictions based your recordings. This is a helpful skill for a kayaker even if you do carry a weather radio. As a kayaker, you will be concerned with weather on a very local level, whereas the weather forecast will always cover a much wider area. If high winds are predicted you should be able to figure out how this weather is going to affect you and your intended route. Pay attention and learn.

Cold fronts are on the leading edge of a cold air mass. Changes are sudden and more violent than a warm front. Squalls, heavy rains and even hail are typical of a cold front. The clouds billow up swiftly to form the spectacular anvil-topped, cumulonimbus clouds. Jagged lightning and ominous rumbling make finding a safe haven off the water an urgent matter. When a cold front approaches, you can feel the temperature dropping, the wind backing and getting stronger. The cloud ceiling lowers. It gives a kayaker little time to take shelter.

Warm fronts, on the other hand, are at the leading edge of a warm air mass pushing a cold air mass. They move more slowly, warm air riding up and over the cold air. High, shadowless cirrus clouds, the ones we call mare's tails, are seen a couple of days ahead of the rain. The altostratus clouds form, and then the lower ones, the stratocumulus clouds, move in with the front. Warm fronts are gentler. These fronts tend to move in with rain expected for a longer period of time.

Fog

On Lake Superior we get used to paddling in fog, especially in the springtime when moisture-laden warm air is blown toward the land across the cold water. This fog is so thick that author Wayland Drew described it as "milk filling a dark green bowl." A wind is needed to break up this fog. On occasion we have traveled all day using only our map, compass and the sound of water against the shore to tell us whether there was a sand beach or a rock cliff close by. Our watch and our experience are the tools we use to help us plot how fast we are moving in this white, sound-muffled space. Wind and tides can certainly add to the challenge of this disorienting experience. If you make a crossing, keep your fellow paddlers in sight and your foghorn handy, and be sure to aim off, to hit the far shore intentionally upstream or downstream of your destination so that once you have crossed, you know exactly which way to turn to reach your destination.

Who Has Seen the Wind?

Wind, rain and tides can both help and hinder our progress on the water. Understanding the particular type of climate you choose to paddle in, and the seasonal weather associated with that climate, will go a long way in helping you make wise decisions on the route you plan, the equipment you use and the people with whom you paddle. Specific types of weather combined with the effects of local topography can affect the kayaker in many ways.

How Topography Affects the Wind

The geography of the coast affects the speed and direction of the wind. Anabatic and katabatic winds are examples of this; corner winds, gap winds and wind spills are other particular kinds of wind resulting from the topography of the land meeting the water. Along the shore of Lake Superior, just as with an ocean coast, the wind can be thought of as its own flowing river moving past obstacles that will serve to both slow it down and speed it up. The friction of the land can slow the flow of wind just as water in a river is slowed along the riverbanks. But then as the wind flows around a corner, that is, an obstacle such as a headland, it speeds up. When wind is funneled through a narrow gap, it speeds up in the same way that water constricted through a narrow gorge suddenly speeds up. When wind spills down a headland, it is like falling water. When it hits the water, these wind spills, or williwaws, can create confused surface conditions. A paddler also has to consider what happens to the wind after it passes an obstacle such as a headland or island. Like water in a river that eddies back upstream behind the obstacle, so too does wind, often creating safe havens of very calm conditions in the lee of islands. Valleys, inlets, steep cliffs and islands alter the wind direction and speed on a very localized level that can be far different from the overall regional weather forecast. For coastal kayakers, it is particularly important to study both topographic maps and marine charts, and to talk to local mariners about treacherous local winds.

A considerable difference in air and water temperature, as happens in the spring and fall, generates fog that can create both mysterious and risky paddling conditions.

Paddling Against the Wind

Paddling against the wind can be frustrating if you don't relax and use plenty of torso rotation with every stroke. Keep paddling through the trough and use a more relaxed stroke on the uphill. Make course corrections at the crest of the wave where the kayak pivots most easily. Pay attention to your technique as there is a common tendency, in the excitement, to speed up the cadence and forget torso rotation. It is important to adjust the cadence of your strokes to take advantage of the pulse of the wind. Paddle a little harder every time the wind lets up a bit. If it is a particularly strong wind and you are near shore, you can take advantage of the fact that the wind is slowed down by any little indentations in the shore and by the vegetation. Paddling close to shore also enables you to determine how much headway you are actually making against the wind.

Paddling in crosswinds is the greatest challenge, as you have to adjust for the two forces acting upon you from different directions; the water below you and the wind above you. Reviewing the Fundamentals of Paddling in Chapter 6, picture your kayak with the wind as a force against it at the side. If you were just sitting still in your kayak, the wind would blow it sideways.

However, as the kayak moves forward, the force of the water is acting upon it as well. Look back at the diagram on forces in Chapter 6, and you will recall that the most water pressure acts upon either side of the kayak from a point where the bow splits the water to the widest point of

the hull. From there back, the stern is actually in the eddy. (Remember, this is why steering strokes are most effective in the stern.) With a crosswind, the downwind (leeward) side of the bow has a lot of pressure on it. Since the stern does not have this kind of pressure on it, the bow tries to swing upwind away from this pressure. (A more rockered hull design will encourage a kayak to weathercock — the bow wants to turn into the wind — even more easily.)

To keep the kayak on a straight course, adjust your stroke so that on the windward (upwind) side you are actually making stronger strokes and partially sweeping. Edge the kayak toward the wind and time your strokes so that you are not planting a forward stroke on the downwind side just as a large wave passes beneath the hull. (A wave can suddenly shove the kayak sideways so it runs over the blade and results in a capsize.) Very strong crosswinds can grab the paddle, especially a wide-bladed, feathered one, right out of your hands. If this happens, don't try to fight

it. Let go with the one hand that controls the upwind blade and then recover. It is also important to make sure that the kayak is well trimmed, because in a bow-heavy kayak, the bow acts like an anchor point and the kayak turns upwind very easily.

Dropping your rudder or skeg creates more lateral pressure at the stern, which enables the kayak to track better. You can even vary the amount of skeg that you wish to drop down. However, a note of caution: Gary and I first took up kayaking in whitewater designs that tracked poorly and spun easily, yet we used them for a lot of lake travel and, in the process, became very aware of what the hull was doing in the wind and how to compensate. Learning this intuitive balance is like taking the training wheels off your bicycle. Learn to paddle comfortably in a wind without using a rudder or skeg so that you are not dependant upon it but rather can simply use it to enhance, and make more comfortable, the effort of staying on course.

WIND

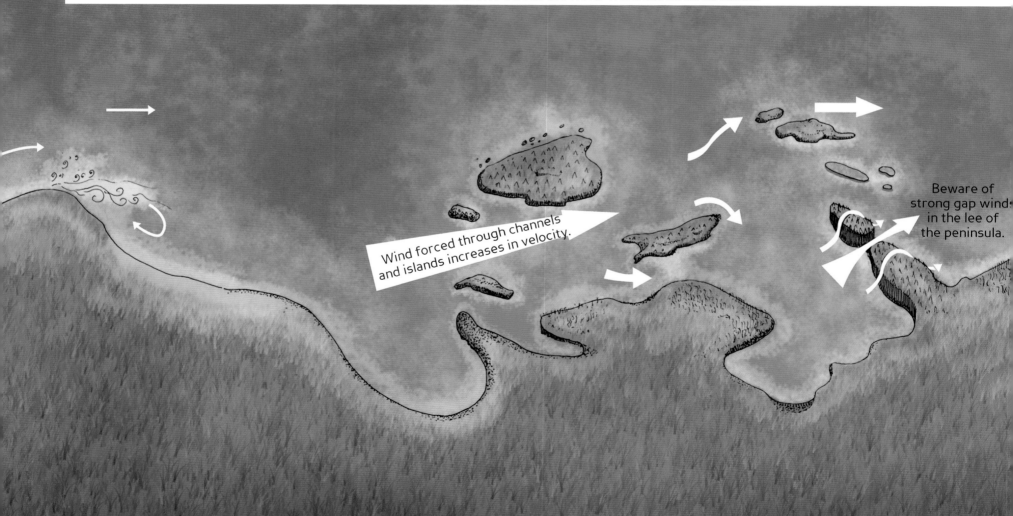

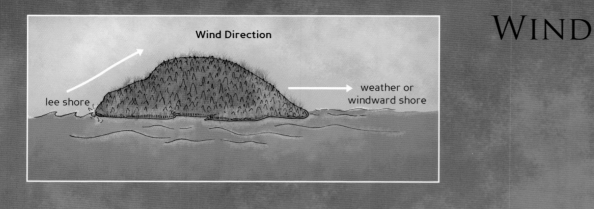

Wind Direction

lee shore

weather or windward shore

FETCH is the distance the wind blows across the water from the same direction.

Wind forced through channels and islands increases in velocity.

Beware of strong gap winds in the lee of the peninsula.

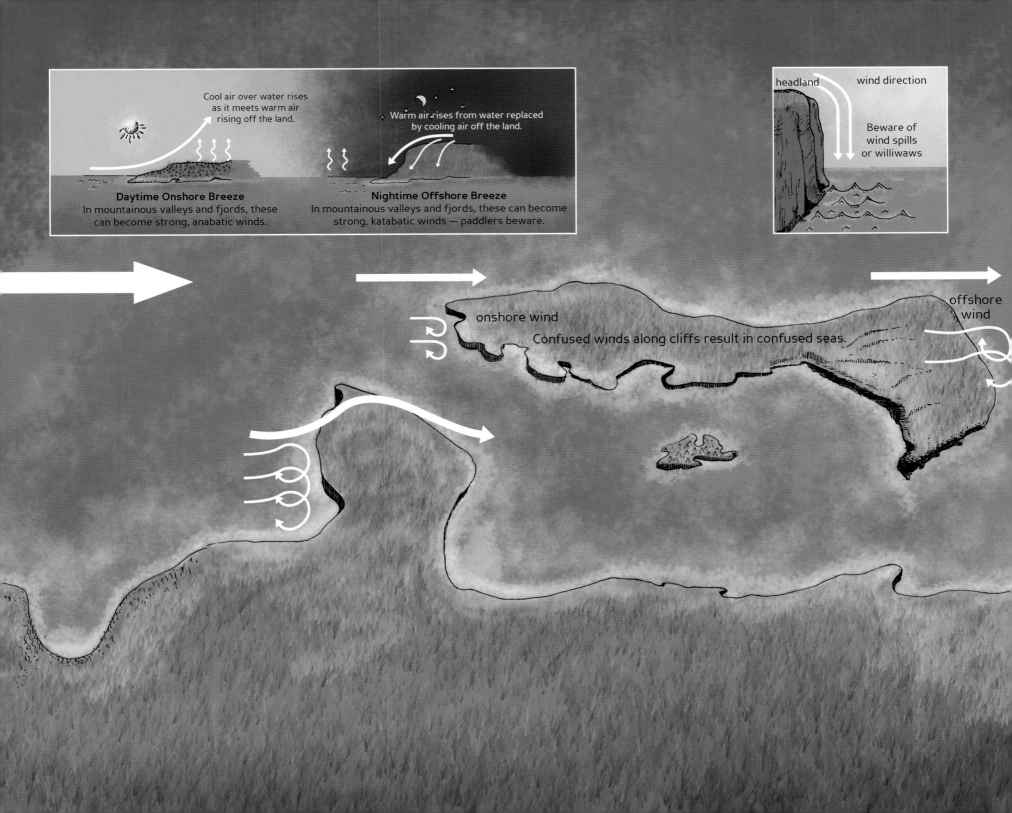

Cool air over water rises as it meets warm air rising off the land.

Daytime Onshore Breeze
In mountainous valleys and fjords, these can become strong, anabatic winds.

Warm air rises from water replaced by cooling air off the land.

Nightime Offshore Breeze
In mountainous valleys and fjords, these can become strong, katabatic winds — paddlers beware.

headland   wind direction

Beware of wind spills or williwaws

onshore wind

Confused winds along cliffs result in confused seas.

offshore wind

Paddling in Wind and Waves

Moving into a wind, whether on a bicycle or in a kayak, often feels like more work than cycling up a mountain or paddling upstream. But with a few tips on body mechanics and boat position, you will find ways to lessen your effort. With efficient technique, you will learn to actually enjoy paddling in the wind!

When you are paddling on a windy day, there are two forces acting upon your kayak. They are the wind itself and the water. Paddling with the wind means that you have the wind to your back. Every paddler loves a tailwind as long as it doesn't change the surface of the water. When that happens, some specific technique is needed so that you do not find yourself wasting energy paddling up the back face of the waves or broaching (turning sideways) in the following seas.

The secret is maintaining momentum, paying attention to your paddling cadence and the rhythm of the waves. Keep the kayak pointed straight ahead, perpendicular to the waves. Look over your shoulder at the approaching wave. As your stern is being lifted, paddle with force to give yourself speed on the downside of the wave. If your bow begins to purl (bury itself), lean back to lift the bow (unless, of course, you want to be pitchpoled!)

CROSSWIND FORCE ON KAYAK WHEN THE KAYAK IS AT REST

wind direction

CROSSWIND AND WATER FORCES ON KAYAK MOVING FORWARD

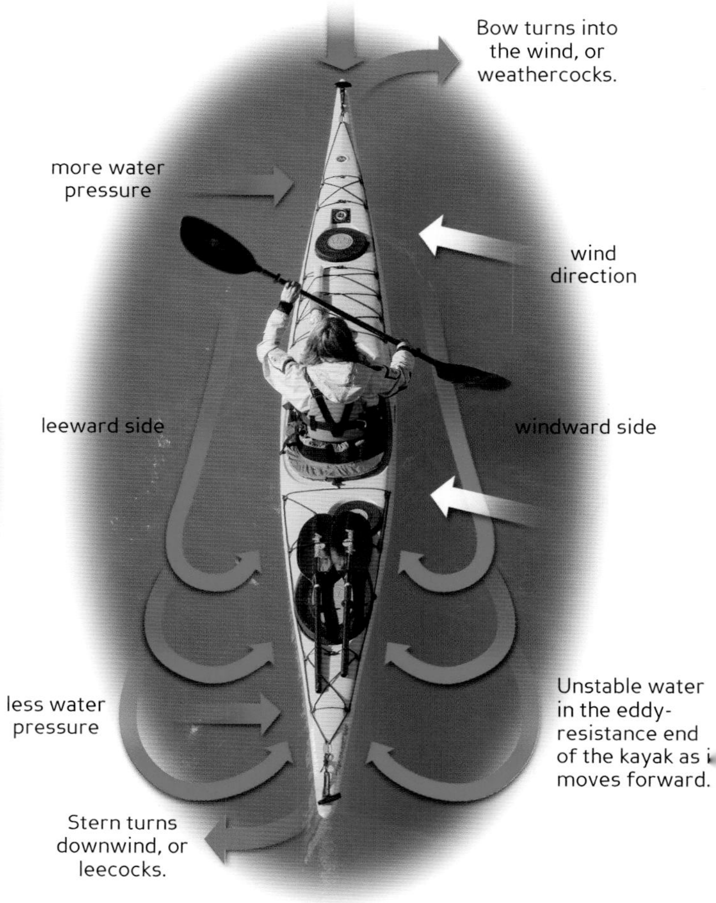

Bow turns into the wind, or weathercocks.

more water pressure

wind direction

leeward side

windward side

less water pressure

Unstable water in the eddy-resistance end of the kayak as it moves forward.

Stern turns downwind, or leecocks.

ABOVE LEFT The force of the wind acting upon a stationary kayak pushes it in the direction in which the wind is blowing as in the diagram. ABOVE RIGHT However, if the kayak is moving forward, the force of the water as well as the wind is acting upon it. When the wind blows from one side, the water pressure against the downwind side of the bow is much stronger than at the stern, so the kayak wants to turn upwind or turn to windward. (See How to View the Illustrations at page 53.)

Waves

Watching water move is endlessly fascinating, whether it is the lazy flow of a river or the march of waves crashing along a sand beach. Of all the different kinds of waves, those brought about by the wind — the whitecaps and swells — are the ones that concern kayakers most. Waves are more predictable than the wind, and once you recognize patterns, you can better gauge how to tackle them, launch in them or avoid them. Three things affect the size of the waves: the fetch (the extent of water over which the wind blows), the length of time the wind is blowing and the wind speed. By looking at your map, you can determine the fetch. You can also anticipate that features such as cliffs can result in rebounding waves, flat beaches mean spilling waves for safe surfing, and steep beaches can mean dangerous plunging breakers. By studying the map and noting the depth and shape of the bottom and shoreline, you can make decisions ahead of time. For instance, you can surmise that if there is a westerly blow and you are beneath some east-facing cliffs, you will be in their lee, under their protection. If you were to cross a channel to a beach, you would know ahead of time that surfing skills were going to be required to get to shore.

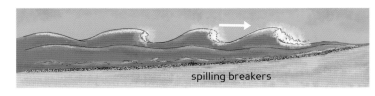

FLAT BEACH

STEEP BEACH

VERY STEEP BEACH

ABOVE The angle of the rising bottom dictates how an approaching wave will break. A gentle rise dissipates the waves' energy over a longer distance, creating the spilling breakers ideal for surfing and safe landings. When the bottom rises quickly, the sudden friction causes the waves to abruptly steepen and the tops fall off, releasing all their power in one big dump. With surging breakers, the wave breaks at shore in a huge foam pile. Also be very wary of steep beaches, for launchings are difficult and landings are dangerous.

LEFT When ice calves from the glacier, it carries with it a story of its time on the land. White, brown and black ones contain snow and earth; clear ones like ice cubes are pure frozen water; and azure blue, the most beautiful of all, have air pockets within that reflect the polar light.

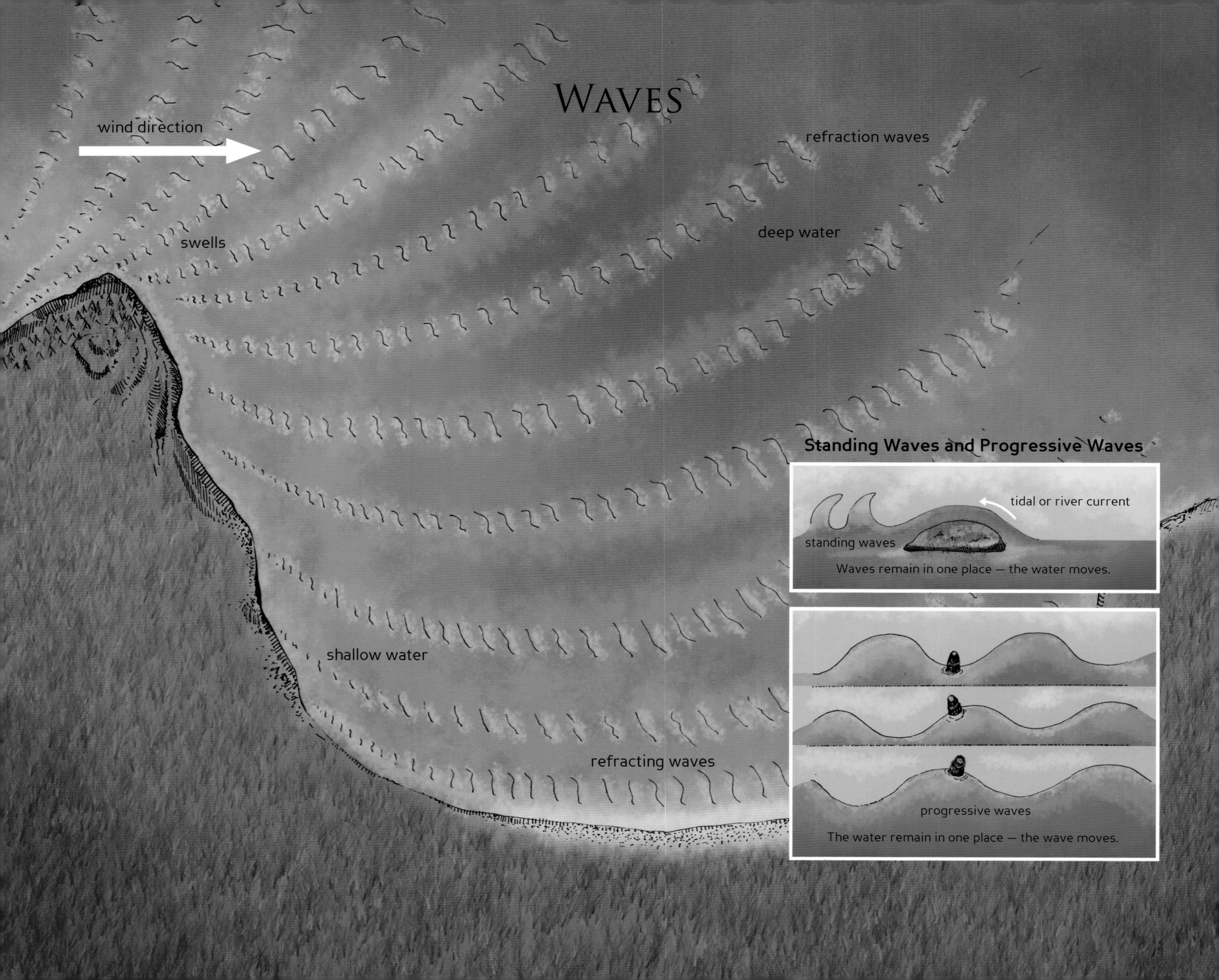

WAVES

wind direction

refraction waves

deep water

swells

shallow water

refracting waves

Standing Waves and Progressive Waves

tidal or river current

standing waves

Waves remain in one place — the water moves.

progressive waves

The water remain in one place — the wave moves.

The Hazards of Headlands

Energy of waves concentrated
at headlands and points.

wind direction

incoming swells

headland

point of land

bay

Energy of waves spread out
and dissipated in the bay.

Rebounding Waves

clapotis

Tides

Where we live on Lake Superior, the water is so vast that it seems like an ocean. Yet unlike the water in an ocean, the water here is not always on the move. When the air is calm, the water is calm. After a storm, the swells will eventually die down and disappear. If you are always going to paddle on inland lakes, even those as extensive as the Great Lakes, you never need to worry about tides. The sea, however, is breathing. Twice a day, the gravitational pull of the moon causes the sea closest to it, and on the opposite side of the earth, to be drawn toward it like a giant magnet. Twice a day, every day, on the oceans, there is a high tide and a low tide. Anyone paddling on the sea needs to know what the tide is doing on that particular day in that exact location.

Unlike other weather patterns that are not so predictable, but like water in a river, tides can be studied. The behavior of tidal water movements around obstacles such as headlands or islands is the same as those of river currents around rocks and along riverbanks. When the tide is rising, it is said to be flooding, and when it is going down, it is said to be ebbing. Twice every month when the moon, sun and earth are aligned, the combined gravitational tidal bulge produces higher high tides and lower low tides. These are known as "spring" tides, and they have the greatest influence on the coastline and the kayakers who explore these shores. During spring tide, the tidal races are much stronger, more violent and run much faster. This energy can be either a help or hindrance to paddlers, depending on which way they are traveling in relation to the tide.

Tide Terminology

APOGEE is when the moon is farthest from the earth and exerts the least lunar influence on the tides.

CURRENT is the horizontal movement of the water. When it is caused by the tide, it is called a tidal current, or tidal stream.

DRIFT is the speed of the tidal current in knots.

EBB is the fall of the tide. When it is going out, the tide is ebbing.

FLOOD is the rising tide. When it comes in, the tide is flooding.

NEAP TIDE is the minimum tidal range for a given area, and it happens when the moon and the sun are at right angles.

OVERFALL is the turbulence caused when a strong tidal current passes through a shallow spot and suddenly drops into deeper water, forming a dangerous standing wave that breaks upstream.

PERIGEE is when the moon is closest to the earth and exerts the greatest lunar influence on the tides.

SET is the direction of tidal current flow. If the tide is flowing east to west, the set is westerly. (It is important to note that when describing wind, we describe it in the opposite direction, that is, a wind blowing east to west is an easterly wind)

SPRING TIDE is the maximum tidal range for a given area. It happens when the sun and the moon are in line with the earth creating the greatest gravitational pull on the ocean. Spring tide has nothing to do with the season of spring.

The **SLACK TIDE**, or **SLACK WATER**, is the period between the flooding and the ebbing tidal currents.

The **TIDE** is the vertical movement of the water that is a result of the gravitation pull of the sun and the moon.

The **TIDE HEIGHT** is the vertical measurement between the surface and the mean low water.

TIDE RIPS is the surface turbulence where tidal current is restricted or forced to sharply change direction.

The **TIDE TABLE** shows the height of the water at a particular location at a particular time and date. The National Ocean Service creates annual tide tables that are a global source of information regarding high and low water.

TIDAL RACE is created where the speed of the tidal flow increases significantly due to topographic features both above and below the water.

At high tide, familiar stopping places will be underwater. At low tide, you have to be wary of now revealed rocks and reefs that the water will flow around, creating their own hazards. When the moon, sun and earth are at right angles to one another, the tidal bulges do not add up to one big pull in one direction, but instead there is a smaller tidal range. These are known as "neap tides," and they occur with the first quarter or last quarter of the moon. The lunar day is 24 hours and 50 minutes. Since the tide changes twice each day, which means two high tides and two low tides, there is a period of 6 hours and 12½ minutes between tidal changes.

The tidal range experienced at any particular location is subject to irregular coastal geography, time in the lunar cycle and the season. In some regions, tidal patterns are accurately recorded and current tables and atlases are available. However, since a kayak is so small and it moves relatively slowly, there will be many times when the actualities of the moment don't match the tide chart because the chart simply can't show such minute detail. The complexities and intricacies of narrow passages and near-shore depth variations, which are so attractive to the kayaker, can cause the tidal bulge to do wild and chaotic things. Tidal bores can be as high as a one-storey house, standing waves can be twice your height, and huge whirlpools can suck you vertically into a spinning vortex. Kayakers often use the back eddies that flow in the direction opposite to the main current (just as one does while paddling upstream on a river). It is important to understand what the water is doing as the back eddy meets the main

current because sooner or later you have to cross this line and it can be very confusing. Tidal currents change four times a day but not necessarily in the opposite direction. The rise and fall of the tide creates a horizontal current that is most pronounced, and most treacherous, in sheltered, restricted coastal passages such as those found in

inland waterways like those off the coast of British Columbia and Alaska.

In addition to a good general understanding of tides and the lunar cycle, you need a keen sense of observation and good record keeping. These attributes greatly assist kayakers in predicting water movements.

Spring Tides and Neap Tides

Third Quarter — Neap Tide

Full Moon — Spring Tide

New Moon — Spring Tide

First Quarter — Neap Tide

When the moon and sun align with the earth, the tidal influence is greatest. This is a spring tide. When the moon and sun are offset, the tidal range is less. This is a neap tide.

TIDES

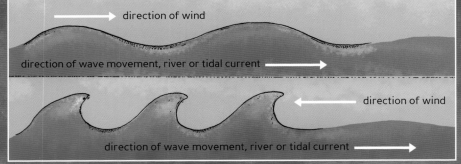

Wind With and Against Current or Water Movement

direction of wind →

direction of wave movement, river or tidal current →

← direction of wind

direction of wave movement, river or tidal current →

Paddlers traveling in areas where there are tides need to familiarize themselves with conditions by reading a tide table, reading nautical charts, carrying a watch and planning ahead to estimate the best route to take and the times to travel it most efficiently and safely in relation to the tide. Experienced local paddlers can be an excellent source of knowledge. Fellow paddlers familiar with the slower speed at which we travel may offer more suitable advice than operators of large motorized vessels. The hazards experienced by a kayaker can be entirely different from those experienced by a watercraft that travels some distance from shore under power. Conversely, what is a safe haven for a kayaker can be completely impossible for a larger vessel to access at all.

incoming swells on a steep beach

plunging surf

longshore current

longshore current

rip current

Beware of River Mouths

incoming swell

steep breaking waves

shallow water due to river sediment

current

whirlpools along eddyline

shoreline eddy

eddyline

midriver eddy

standing waves

midriver eddy

downstream V

direction of current

rock garden

rip tide

standing waves

direction of tidal current

tide rips

CHAPTER 13

PLANNING YOUR OWN ADVENTURE

YOU HAVE DECIDED THAT YOU HAVE HAD ENOUGH of playing in your own little paddling pool and you want to go somewhere new. When you are planning for an adventure, be it a day, a week or a month long, you have to make some particular and significant decisions before you go anywhere.

How long is this adventure going to be? Is it a daytrip or longer? Is it close to home or far away? Is it a trip that will be organized by an outfitter or one that you will organize yourself? What skills do you need to undertake this? Be realistic about your capabilities. What is the focus of the trip?

The last question is an important one that is often overlooked. You can have the best weather, gear and food, but if the people don't have the same aspirations, the trip can be a real ordeal. Some paddlers like to beeline it from point to point with the challenge of speed and distance covered being of uppermost importance. For others, the kayak is the means to access remote fishing places, a vehicle to get from one great campsite to another, or a place from which to birdwatch or skin dive.

Recently we were on a journey accompanied by fellow artists on Lake Superior's north shore. Although our paddling and camping skills varied from beginner to advanced, the important thing among us was our love for interpreting the landscape through photography and painting. We didn't mind traveling

When planning an adventure, don't forget the special treats you can make around the campfire or enjoy on a stormy day, like toasting marshmallows or baking bannock.

slowly or spontaneously changing our plans to explore a bay that looked suitable for observing moose. If there had been one or two among us who were speed demons, there could have been a fair amount of strife. Much depends on the reasons you are out there in the first place. On one trip, our goal was to paddle across Canada from the Atlantic to the Arctic Ocean in two seasons. We knew we were racing against winter and freeze-up and so traveling each day was important. When our daughter came into our lives, we planned adventures where we were not the least bit concerned about distance and speed. Our focus became her enjoyment of the places we so loved. We traveled with a child's perspective, paddling close to shore, swimming a lot, building sandcastles and beachcombing.

Deciding Where to Go

The possibilities appear boundless, yet we think as 21st-century paddlers we belong to a special community of people who have a responsibility to the waterways and coastlines. We need to give some serious consideration to what the impact of our actions will be on the region we want to explore. Asking ourselves whether flying to a particular destination is really worth the overall environmental cost is a hard question unique to our time in history. And considering whether our paddling adventure has been of positive benefit to the wildlife, the people, the local economy and culture of the region is of increasing importance if we care about more than our personal pleasure.

On a practical level, begin by gathering as much information as possible about the area you want to visit. Pore over the maps, research places through guidebooks and the internet (but always double-check to make sure your sources are reliable), frequent your bookstore for good literature from the region, and seek out historical stories of the area you are interested in. If possible, talk to local paddlers. Local outfitters, outdoor shops and paddling clubs are all places to find paddlers who may know the practical side of

A large mesh bag with a waterproof bottom is an ideal solution for carrying your mountain of little bags from your car to your kayak and from your kayak to your campsite. Pack sleeping bags, clothing and dried food in waterproof compression stuff sacs.

traveling in a certain region, especially with regard to the weather, tides, and manmade and natural hazards.

Consider a guided experience into a new area. First-time trips into a region are often best tackled with a good local outfitter who knows people and how to teach well, knows what to expect along the route, knows how to keep a group of people safe and comfortable, and knows and respects nature and the local wildlife, people and customs.

You also need to consider your physical condition and your personal experience. Will you need to be concerned about carrying freshwater? Are you looking at a wilderness trip where you will make your own camps along the way, or are there designated camping places such as in the parks or along water trails? (Official water trails, varying in length from a few miles to a few hundred miles, usually have a system of designated campsites intended for small watercraft.) Do you like warm or cool temperatures? Consider potential seasonal weather hazards such as high winds, rain or extreme heat and how you will prepare for these conditions.

Get detailed maps and charts for the area you are going to be covering. Study them. Identify the places you would like to go and examine land and water features. If applicable, consider the effects of tides based on up-to-date tidal charts. This will help you determine access points, and launching and landing places. Plot a variety of courses considering wind and weather changes and unexpected events with paddlers and equipment. Think about open-water crossings carefully. Preplanning is especially helpful as a safety consideration. Reviewing the maps is a way of becoming more intimate with the area beforehand. The exercise turns a two-dimensional map into a three-dimensional picture in your mind, taking you places before you even leave home. An example would be looking at the contours on the shoreline that describe a stretch of cliffs dropping straight to the water's edge. On the one hand, if the weather is calm and fair, paddling beneath those towering cliffs would be a trip highlight. But if caught there in the wind, depending on your skill level, the paddling conditions could be very risky indeed.

ABOVE It is important to agree on the reasons for your journey in the planning stages. For us, keeping meals simple gives us time for photography, painting and playing with Sila.

Loading a Kayak

A well organized and packed kayak means the difference between your kayak performing well or not, and your having the ability to find things when you need them. Over the years we have learned that developing a packing system that you can always use is key to saving time and avoiding frustration. Organizing food is a challenge and there are many ways of handling this, from daily rations to breakfast, lunch and supper ingredient bags. Lay out everything that needs to be packed into the kayak. There will be a variety of shapes and sizes, from small compressible items such as clothing to long, large items such as the tent, awkward pots and kitchen utensils, and sometimes very heavy containers of drinking water. As you pack, distribute the weight evenly from bow to stern and side to side so that you are neither bow nor stern heavy, nor are you listing to one side.

ABOVE It is hard to believe how much you can actually stuff into a tandem and a solo kayak. When you pack efficiently, these two kayaks will swallow up to three weeks' worth of food and supplies with no trouble at all. All your safety and rescue equipment including your PFDs, paddle floats, pump, rescue sling and spare paddle are readily available. Deck bags are very handy for storing the items you use throughout the day such as water bottles, sunscreen, cameras, binoculars and snacks.

LEFT Kayaks have to be packed with small stuff sacs of various shapes and sizes in order to maximize the use of the space. When packing all this gear in, consider keeping long shapes toward the ends, big and bulky ones in the larger stern compartment, and weighty items over the centerline. Among the items laid out here are paddles, a bilge pump, sponge, rescue throwline, the PFDs, clothing stuff sacs, sleeping pads, sleeping bags, maps and books in a waterproof case, the tent, camp shoes, the stove, kitchen utensils and food bags, first-aid kit, repair kit, fishing tackle, wash basin, waterbags, sprayskirts, cockpit covers and camera packs.

The stuff sacs containing sleeping bags, sleeping pads, clothing and the tent have been further unpacked to demonstrate that although you can carry a lot in your kayak, you need to know where everything is. To do this, use different colored stuff sacs for different items then consistently pack the same things in the same stuff sacs. If you do not do this, you will be endlessly searching for things. The safety, rescue, first aid and repair kits need to be identifiable and easily accessible. Lunches, snacks and any clothing such as raingear also need to be close at hand. We all develop our own packing style and no one way is best.

Dry Bags and Deck Bags

As a kayaker, you are wise to have a selection of dry bags in all shapes and sizes. They are made of vinyl or urethane-coated nylon (more abrasion resistant) and, if closed properly, are completely watertight. Choose a clear one for your VHF radio and another for your flare kit. When you are packing for a longer trip, you will quickly see why different shapes are useful—long and narrow ones for the sleeping pads and tent and shorter ones for sleeping bags and clothing. With them, you are able to squeeze out all the air, compressing the contents and making best use of the available space in your kayak.

RIGHT, TOP A selection of dry bags. The red bag in the foreground has a drysuit zipper and the inflatable bladder acts as padding and flotation for carrying fragile equipment such as cameras. The large yellow one on the left is a contoured dry bag that, once filled and sealed, can be inflated thereby acting as dry storage and added flotation. All the rest, of varying sizes and shapes, have roll-down closures that make convenient carrying handles. Use the colors as code to differentiate clothing from sleeping/tenting gear and so on. The one on the right in the foreground is a transparent bag that enables you to see its contents.

RIGHT Three different deck bags, with different capabilities. The one on the white kayak is totally waterproof; a drysuit zipper seals the opening, thereby making it suitable for carrying camera equipment. The large-volume contoured deck bag on the orange kayak has numerous attachment points for maps, and a zippered mesh pouch. It is water resistant. The one on the yellow kayak is a lower-volume more contoured, water-resistant bag. Both fasten with an ordinary zipper and are water repellant.

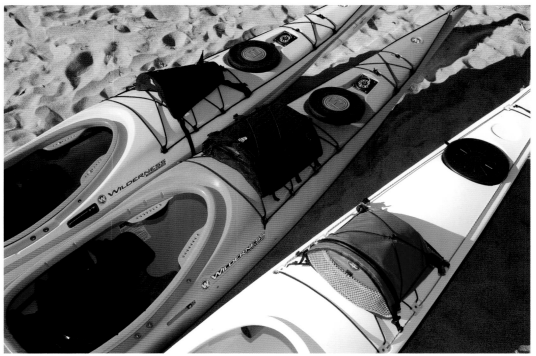

Extending the Frontier

For some, extending the frontier means to "go where no one has gone before," but for most of us, it is simply finding ways to incorporate the things we really love to do into busy lives.

For some, thoughts of paddling a kayak have been curtailed because of something as simple as owning a faithful canine companion that goes everywhere with you. Others may have small children and be discouraged by the thought of the expense of one or two tandem kayaks, but still want to find a way to share the experience. Others may just want to add a new dimension to the familiar.

We have watched over the years as the variety of gear and gadgets for paddlers has increased exponentially. You can certainly get carried away with all the "product" available, but there are a number of clever inventions that can provide real pleasure and convenient ways to expand your kayaking experience. Among them, we consider these particularly worth trying: the KayRak, with or without sail rig, and the Trak folding kayak.

An incredible 150-mile section of Great Lakes coast links two of Canada's most beautiful parks, Lake Superior Provincial Park and Pukaskwa National Park. Here, near Otter Island lighthouse, where the Cascade River tumbles into the lake, we are camped at the most remote point of the entire Great Lakes, a remarkable setting considering the huge number of populous communities within a day's drive of the parks.

Outriggers

At one point in our life together, Gary and I acquired a beautiful Alaskan malamute. Up until she was a year old, she was content to crawl into the cockpit, where she would curl up between Gary's legs. It amazed us that she was even content to have the sprayskirt on the kayak. But Kalija outgrew the space and a canoe was much more comfortable for journeys with her through those years. Then our family grew with the birth of our daughter, Sila, and a canoe continued for three more years as our paddling craft of choice. But we did meet a lot of people asking questions about paddling with dogs and children and whether we had ever come across a solution to this dilemma. Then we met Bart Boelryk and his KayRak. He had designed this platform to which you can attach one or two outriggers purely for the benefit of taking his dog along on the adventure, too. It is an ingenious and well-designed piece of equipment that is simple to install. Sila has enjoyed daytrips aboard the KayRak, especially when we have brought along the sail rig shown at right. There are any number of applications for this stable kayaking platform, not least of which is opening up the kayaking world for people whose disabilities would require this kind of stabilizing support to participate in the sport.

It works better on a kayak with a rudder as you can no longer edge the kayak to turn it. But the beauty of it is its versatility and the fact that it can be adapted to any kayak. Even the platform can be removed instantly so you have access to your rear hatch.

Adding a platform and an outrigger to the kayak was Bart Boelryk's ingenious solution to the problem of how to take his canine companion along. The outrigger provides further waterproof storage as well as great stability. It has any number of uses including that of a concert stage and diving platform.

Sail Rig

One summer when I was growing up, my father purchased a sail kit with outriggers that could be attached to our family's cedar canvas canoe. My brother, sister and I were given the freedom to sail and canoe on the bay all alone without adults aboard. Many July afternoons were spent aboard our magic canoe bringing alive the adventures of my favorite sailing stories of traveling around the world. You can fashion a quick little sail to catch a tailwind simply by taking your spare breakdown paddle apart and threading the shaft of each piece up through the body of a T-shirt and into the sleeves. It is simple and fun but your arms quickly tire from holding up your temporary sail.

The beauty of the manufactured sail rig shown here is that it is virtually hands-free. The apparatus does not require that any hardware be affixed to the kayak as the existing deck rigging suffices. It is the tension of the lines that holds the sail in place. For those who love sailing, for families with young children and dogs, and for people with physical challenges, the KayRak and the sail rig are fun additions that expand the use of your kayak and open up paddling opportunities that might not otherwise exist.

This simple, well-designed sail rig needs only the tension of lines attached to existing deck rigging to hold it in place. With the platform and outriggers in place, a lot of stability has been added, not to mention a place for a child or dog to accompany you on your adventure. The sail rig collapses quickly for easy transportation. And if the wind hits it hard, the sail will collapse momentarily spilling excess wind instead of tipping you over. The whole rig can be stored on the deck of the kayak when not in use.

Folding Kayaks

We have used folding kayaks very successfully on trips where the remoteness of the location made the cost of transporting a hard-shell kayak prohibitive. They are also an option for someone who has limited storage space. Stowaway kayaks are carried in their own backpack, which can be transported as luggage on an airline or floatplane, or hiked overland to a remote lake or inaccessible put-in point. The concept of a frame with a skin has been around a long time. Originally the Inuit built their kayaks from driftwood frames lashed and pegged together then covered with seal, caribou or walrus skin. They were not, however, designed to be taken apart and repacked again and again as modern skin-on-frame kayaks are.

We now have frames of a lightweight aluminum alloy inserted into a Cordura and Hypalon skin. The particular kayak shown here has a shock-corded frame so, unlike other collapsible kayaks, which are a bit of a puzzle with numerous pieces to assemble, this one only takes a few minutes. Today folding (and inflatable) kayaks open up the paddling world to people who would like to go kayaking but who have neither the space to store one nor the automobile to car-top one.

1 The whole kayak fits in a large duffle bag, allowing for easy storage, roof-rack free transportation and less expensive flights into remote areas.

2 Unzip the bag and lay out the shell, cockpit rim, seat and the frame sections.

6 The stern frame section is in place.

7 Insert and connect the cockpit coaming.

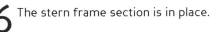

3 On the Trak kayak, the great advantage is that the frame is shock-corded together in only two sections. Just shake them out, attach two ribs each to the bow and stern sections.

4 Insert the bow frame assembly into the shell.

5 Note the three hydraulic jacks laid out on the seat ready to install. These provide a unique system in the Trak kayak that will allow the frame's rocker to be altered while underway.

8 The three hydraulic jacks are inserted into the frame. They are cranked up, thereby forcing the frame assembly into the ends and tightening up the shell. The deck rigging is fastened into place.

9 The seat is placed in the kayak, seat pillars connected to the frame, and the backrest cords attached to allow for seat-back adjustment. The closure on the stern deck of the kayak, called the keeder, is sealed. The jacks are used to further tighten the shell.

10 After a couple of run-throughs to familiarize yourself with the process, assembly of this take-apart kayak takes ten minutes or less. (Note the removable deck-mounted compass attached with bungee cords which can be fastened to any kayak's deck rigging.)

CHAPTER 14

TYING IT ALL TOGETHER

A PARTICULAR KNOT TIED CORRECTLY and used for the job it was intended for is a wonderful thing. One of our favorite books, *The Ashley Book of Knots*, is a bible of some 4,000 knots. The greatest variety were developed aboard ship at sea when sailors had time, a lot of rope, and a practical application to which the finished masterpiece might be applied. We use most of these knots all the time. They represent the major knot categories: bends (rope to rope), hitches (rope to something else) and loop knots. These are the bowline, butterfly, clove hitch, fisherman's knot, traveler's hitch and sheet bend. We have augmented this list with other useful ones for more specific jobs. Knot tying is just sheer fun, but in kayaking, the use of a correctly tied knot could be of life-preserving importance.

Brisk headwinds are hardly a difficulty for the low profile of the kayaker who practices proper technique. It is advisable, however, to tie down loose gear, anchor your tent well, and use a quick clove hitch to secure your kayak to shore.

Double Figure Eight
If the rope is doubled up, a very safe loop is created. Although it can be difficult to untie, it does hold slippery, synthetic rope well.

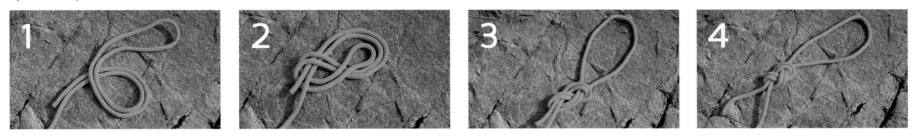

Bowline
The bowline bend is the knot we use more than any other. You can create this very secure loop with one hand and wearing a blindfold. It will not slip yet it undoes easily. Make the rabbit hole, bring the rabbit up the hole, run it around the tree and back down the hole.

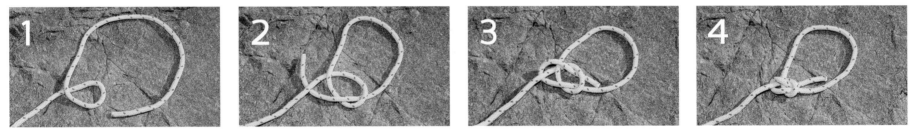

Butterfly
Use the butterfly whenever you need a nonslip loop, or loops, in the middle of a rope. The butterfly is a secure knot that allows a load to be placed on it in any direction, and it is fairly easy to undo. It can secure your kayak to the top of your vehicle. Twist rope into an eight as shown, fold the top loop down and back up through the bottom of the eight.

Taut Line Rolling Hitch

We use the taut line rolling hitch on all our tent guy lines. This hitch slides freely until a load is placed on it, thus allowing you to quickly adjust your guy lines to suit the best place to peg out the tent fly.

Prusik Loop

Take a Prusik loop (created with the fisherman's knot) and attach it (as shown) to the middle of another rope that is thicker in diameter. The Prusik will tighten under pressure yet loosen when tension is released. This is useful for when you need a loop that can be moved along a line, instead of the butterfly loops, which are fixed. It was once called the lineman's knot because you can use it to create a series of loops on a rope, enabling you to climb it.

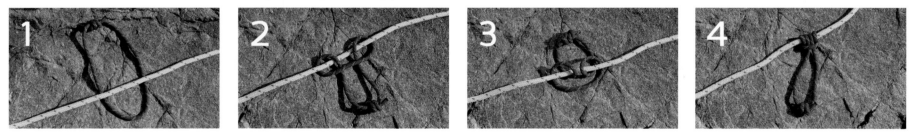

Anchor Bend

The anchor bend was originally used to secure the anchor ring on sailing vessels, which attests to its great strength. This bend will not slip or jam, is useful for mooring a boat, securing a carabiner to a line or a lure to fishing line.

Clove Hitch

The clove hitch is simple and quick to construct and untie. It does not provide bombproof security, but for any job requiring you to fasten a rope to a pole or post such as mooring your kayak at the dock, it is one of the most useful. You can add a couple of half hitches to increase security.

Figure Eight Joining Two Ropes Together

A figure eight can be used to fasten two ropes together: make a figure eight in one rope and then use the other rope to trace this eight, thereby joining the two together.

Fisherman's Knot

Sometimes we use this knot to tie two ropes together. It works particularly well for tying the two ends of a short length of rope together to create a Prusik loop.

Sheet Bend Fastening Two Ropes

The sheet bend is a great bend for fastening two ropes together, especially two ropes of different thicknesses, or rope made of slippery polypropylene. The free ends must be on the same side in order for the sheet bend to be reliable.

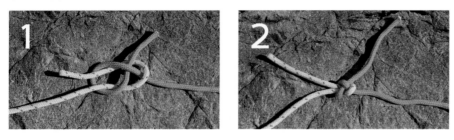

Sheet Bend Joining Two Ropes with a Quick-Release Half Hitch

If you want to fasten two ropes yet have them come apart quickly, finish the sheet bend with a quick-release (slippery) half hitch.

Water Knot

The water knot ties two pieces of flat webbing together in a secure way. Keep the knot neat by tracing the path of the first piece (yellow) with the second piece (green), making sure the webbing stays flat and does not twist.

Daisy Chain

We used to use the daisy chain to moor our kayaks to the dock but the clove hitch or anchor bend is faster for this purpose. We now daisy-chain our towing line for easy stowage in a waist pouch. The line can be peeled out to whatever length is necessary and then tied off. (See Towing Equipment in Chapter 9.)

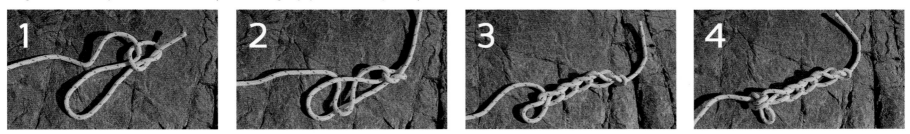

Traveler's Hitch

The traveler's hitch, or power cinch, is a quick method for tying and untying kayaks on vehicles or trailers. This is actually a combination knot that creates a powerful pulley. It is a great knot for cinching down a load. We installed eye bolts to the vehicle frame under the hood then attached two loops to the bolts giving us a secure tie-down for the bow.

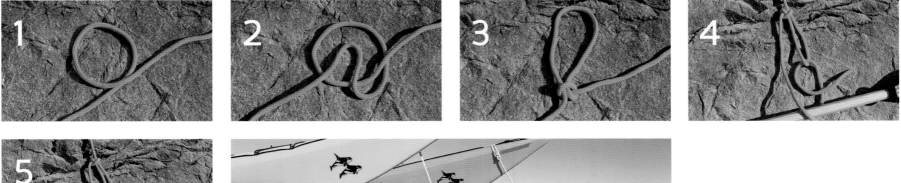

CHAPTER 15

BUILDING YOUR OWN KAYAK

ONE OF THE VERY FIRST EXPERIENCES Gary and I had in our life together was building fiberglass whitewater kayaks. Over the course of several days, we completed our hand-built watercraft. Soon we were proudly packing them up with a weekend or week's worth of supplies and paddling off on many an adventure. Years later, our fondness for this experience was rekindled while visiting Grand Marais in Minnesota's wonderful North House Folk School, where you can learn everything from traditional basket-making to square timber construction. Peter Pestolozzi, a friend and frequent builder of Greenland kayaks, introduced us to the stitch-and-glue construction method. The responsive feel of his handmade kayaks reminded us of our experiences paddling birchbark canoes and, like bark canoes, these kayaks felt light yet very strong, as if they were meant to be traveled in. The idea of starting with flat sheets of plywood and transforming them into our very own custom-built kayaks was exciting to contemplate. We made arrangements to return that autumn to North House Folk School to build kayaks with Peter.

The series of captioned images that follow over the next few pages are meant to provide you with enough step-by-step detail so that you understand what is involved in the process. (If you want to build your own kayak and for more information, look into the Selected Reading and Resources at the end of this book.)

We got started on a crisp October day in the North House woodworking shop. Long wooden workbenches ran along two walls. Windows provided an inspiring view over the Grand Marais harbour and Lake Superior. We could hardly imagine a finer place in which to be undertaking this boatbuilding adventure. A table saw and band saw were close at hand, although more than half of the work would be done with hand tools. Peter had gathered together the necessary materials: marine plywood, epoxy resin, fiberglass cloth and hardware such as the skeg. All were laid out on one work bench, with hand tools, ready to begin.

The workshop was soon a hive of activity. First we customized Peter's existing patterns to suit our own needs. Gary needed to accommodate photographic gear within the cockpit, so he increased its width and depth. He also increased the overall length to 19 feet so

Around spring equinox, when the lake is calm, we celebrate the return of the light by venturing out on our first paddle of the season. On this particular afternoon, the silence was interrupted only by the drip drip drip of melting ice.

as not to sacrifice hull speed. I, in turn, made adjustments to scale down the measurements so that the kayak would fit my smaller size like a glove. Time flew by as we set about measuring and cutting, sawing and sanding, gluing and stitching, fiberglassing and painting. Under the watchful eye of an experienced builder, the two kayaks took fourteen full days from start to finish.

While we built the kayaks our conversation would drift back and forth between present and past. One moment we were discussing the finer points of creating smooth fillets — the joins at the seams — and the next we were contemplating life among the Inuit, particularly the building of traditional qajaq, a "hunter's boat." Once in a while stepping back to admire the evolution of our own little craft, we marveled at the shape, a shape so appropriate for the environment out of which it was born. These narrow, low-volume craft with little rocker, a small cockpit, upturned ends and hard chines were built to the specifications of a particular hunter's measurements (the width of the hips plus two fists and three arm spans long), just as these were built to ours. Those early kayaks made from driftwood frames lashed and pegged together then covered with seal skin performed a kind of magic, transforming a man into a being whose skills at sea were surpassed only by the marine mammals themselves.

We can only remotely imagine what the relationship was between a hunter and his qajaq. The time spent building the kayak is a time of contemplation, and it is with a great sense of pride that you pack up a kayak you built yourself. When you first set your kayak upon the water, slip into it and paddle away from shore, the realization that you are afloat in something that you constructed with your own hands is a wonderful thing. As you paddle along, you find you have a deeper appreciation for all that has gone into the evolution of this craft. As you head out on an adventure, your kayak takes on a life of its own, gathering stories from the places you travel.

It is only natural that we are drawn to faces in nature wherever we paddle. They can be found in gnarled tree trunks, rock formations and even hummocks of ice.

1 Customizing an existing design to suit our needs. We took measurements for adjustments to be made in the overall length, and the width and depth of the cockpit.

2 The kayak was made up of three pattern pieces for the garboards (the underside of the hull) and three patterns for the side planks. There were two 8-foot sections, the stern and the middle, and one smaller section for the bow.

3 The 8-foot lengths of plywood had to be scarfed, or spliced, together in order to accommodate the full length (18 and 19 feet) of the finished kayak hulls.

4 At the places where the side plank stern joins the side plank middle, and the side plank middle joins the side plank bow, the marine plywood can be cut with a utility knife.

5 The pieces for both the garboards and the side planks are cut and labeled for scarfing. We started with twelve pieces of plywood: eight 8-foot sections and four shorter ones. These were spliced together to create two garboards and two side planks, each one being the full length of the finished kayak.

6 Once the splicing is complete, the garboards and the side planks can be cut out and fiberglassed with a 3-ounce cloth and epoxy resin. The bulkheads, hatch flanges and deck pieces are cut out and fiberglassed at the same time.

7 The side planks and garboards are cut out with a jigsaw. You will end up with two garboards that are mirror images of one another, and two side planks which are also exact opposites.

8 Drill holes in the garboards for stitching the keel and the seam together. The bottom edge of the garboard is the keel line. The two garboards are sandwiched fiberglassed sides together and stitched along this line with plastic ties (foreground).

9 The side planks are carefully matched up with the holes along the top edge of the garboards and drilled. The garboards and side planks are stitched forming the chine, then the ends are fitted together, drilled and stitched as well.

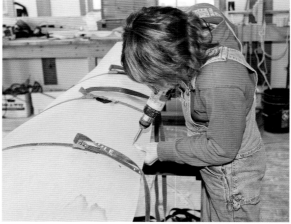

13 Before making the decks, you have to screw in a temporary bulkhead to support the curve at the front of the cockpit coaming. Extra care must be taken, using a level and tape measure, to ensure that the bulkhead is not distorting the kayak anywhere and that the shape remains fair.

14 The triangle-shaped deck pieces cut out and glassed earlier can now be placed on the kayak glassed side down. The whole assembly is strapped together with webbing to hold it in place while you screw it down. The deck is temporarily screwed to the inwales.

15 The hatch openings are located along the centerline of the decks. Center and screw down the pattern, and router out the openings. Pre-glassed, pre-trimmed hatch rings are fitted inside the opening, held with clamps and tacked into place with epoxy.

10 As the stitching takes place, the plywood takes on the beautiful flowing lines of a finished kayak. The bulkhead is used to hold the shape. Snug up the ties, add more ties if necessary, and ensure the overall lines of the kayak are fair.

11 The joints connecting the various garboard, side and bulkhead pieces of plywood are now filleted with a mixture of epoxy, wood flour and silica. Done carefully, this provides a smooth, strong curve on the inside of the joints over which your fiberglass tape can be placed.

12 Following a 12-hour drying period, the plastic ties are cut off with diagonal cutters. The filleted inside seams are sanded as smooth as possible. Fiberglass tape is cut and glassed in along all these seams to complete the necessary strong joint between garboards, side planks and bulkheads.

16 A sandwich of four plywood rings creates the riser for the cockpit opening. Put a clamp on the rear centerline and then one at the front centerline. Then add clamps evenly around the cockpit opening.

17 Short-strand fiberglass-reinforced filler is used to fill in the space between the flange and the deck. The clamps are removed, the filler is mixed and the process has to be completed quickly. It takes several layers of filling, drying, scraping, filling, drying and sanding.

18 The deck is carefully measured and marked for a total of fourteen recessed fittings, then unscrewed from the hull and laid on the workhorses with the underside facing upward. The deck and coaming are cleaned and the recessed fittings attached with epoxy and screws.

19 The skeg is installed very carefully, using a level to make sure it is perfectly aligned with the centerline and that it is square with the hull (not tipped to one side or the other).

20 A length of fiberglass or Kevlar cloth is cut out to cover the entire length of the kayak along the keel line. The resin is applied with a roller.

21 The surface of the underside of the deck must be cleaned, sanded, and any lumps removed so that the fiberglass cloth, placed to reinforce the area around the hatches and the cockpit, will bond.

25 The entire hull is thoroughly sanded. All the little holes around the hatch openings and cockpit coaming are filled and sanded smooth in preparation for painting the deck (a persnickety job), and then the hull.

26 The deck fittings are drilled and finished off in preparation for the deck rigging.

27 The carrying toggles are attached bow and stern.

22 The cloth is cut out at the cockpit and hatch openings. White pigment is added to the fiberglass. This is left to cure while you return to work on the hull.

23 The underside of the deck and the hull lying side by side.

24 The inside of the deck and hull are painted with two coats to seal the wood. A layer of epoxy and wood flour is spread along the top edge of the hull. The deck is then screwed back together and left to dry twelve hours.

28 The deck bungees (black) and deck lines (blue) are threaded into place.

29 The custom seat is cut from closed-cell foam.

30 The prepainted seat blocks are installed.

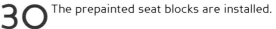

31 The seat is glued in with contact cement. Foot braces are installed. We made custom foot braces by placing a closed-cell foam block up against the bow bulkhead which was originally installed at the correct leg length.

32 The drop-down skeg, and cable for the skeg are installed.

33 Getting the skeg to operate smoothly can be a finicky job, but it is satisfying when all the details of your custom kayak such as the skeg, the seat and the cockpit fit like a glove and work well for you.

Custom building your own kayak means that the kayak is just right for you.

This Inuit hunter is performing in a rolling competition near the capital, Nuuk. There is growing participation in the heritage of building and paddling qajaqs. The small blade under his deck rigging is an aid used in some of the many possible rolls.

CHAPTER 16

PADDLE YOUR OWN KAYAK

WE ARE ALL TRAVELERS IN SPACE AND TIME on one little planet three-quarters covered by water. It is entirely natural that we should be drawn to this life-sustaining medium. The kayak is a vehicle for water experiences, from little lakes to the wide, blue ocean. Just looking at a kayak's elegant, purposeful lines stirs within us that magical desire for discovery of nature and new places. The thoughtful traveler immediately turns to the matter of how, why and where.

Leaving "no trace" is an oft-heard term. It begins with an overall attitude of respect in your home life and how you think about water, air, food and fuel. It means that whenever you look at water you think of it as something that makes up 70 percent of your own body.

It means that when you are contemplating the sky, you begin to see it as something that touches the earth; in this ocean of air is found the very breath of life from the moment you are born until you die. It is a way of looking at the trees and plants, the animals, insects and birds and seeing them as fellow creatures whose lives are dependent upon the places which we may at first just recognize as a holiday playground. A river, a lake, or a seacoast is part of the vast, interconnected web of life and each place has its own fragility and balance that we can help to preserve. Each particular environment has its own

In an age when society has distanced people from the natural world, kayaking bridges that gap wherever there is water to float upon. It is imperative to take children on these adventures if they are to grow up conscious of their relationship with the earth.

code of conduct and it is up to each of us as responsible paddlers to do what is necessary to safeguard the water quality, preserve the aesthetic beauty and follow the necessary protocol established for a particular area.

Read up on no-trace camping and low-impact travel so you can be knowledgeable about the day-to-day decisions you make and the impact they may have. Understand what the recommended practices are and incorporate them into your routine. Learn as much as you can about the wildlife of the region. The environments we paddle through are home to a wealth of life, from small insects to large mammals; most we will not see but our actions will affect their lives. Carry binoculars and field guides so that you can be observant yet respectful. Keep your distance from nests and young animals, and make every precaution to avoid conflict with animals by knowing their seasonal habits and being clean campers.

As paddlers, we can make a positive difference, and not just by using low-impact practices in the places we paddle through. We can also be peaceful warriors in our fight for these places. We can be involved in the conservation of these special places through volunteering with local land trusts, by participating in the development of water trails, finding out about species at risk and endangered species and how to help them, and volunteering to do work for habitat protection. Passion for this kind of work begins by understanding that wildlife, wild places and wilderness are not something separate from our lives. If you begin to discover your own special places close to home, and you share these places kayaking with friends and family, you do not need to look far to find some human-induced threat. See the list of organizations in the Resources section, next, and check out their websites or, better yet, contact them. They will give you ideas to think about and act on. The important thing is to learn about the issues, get involved and volunteer for projects close to your home and your heart.

Coldwell Peninsula, Lake Superior.

SELECTED READING AND RESOURCES

Adventure Kayak magazine.

Alderson, Doug. *Sea Kayaker's Savvy Paddler: More Than 500 Tips for Better Kayaking*. Camden ME: Ragged Mountain Press, 2001.

Alderson, Doug and Michael Pardy. *Handbook of Safety and Rescue*. Camden ME: Ragged Mountain Press, 2003.

Ashley, Clifford W., and Geoffrey Budsworth. *The Ashley Book of Knots*. New York: Doubleday, 1993.

Burch, David. *Fundamentals of Kayak Navigation*, Third Edition. Guilford CT: Globe Pequot Press, 1999.

Canoe & Kayak magazine.

Dowd, John. *Sea Kayaking: A Manual for Long-Distance Touring*. Seattle: University of Washington Press, 1997.

Dyson, George. *Baidarka, The Kayak*. Bothell WA: Alaska Northwest Books, 1986.

Forward Stroke Clinic [Video]. Produced by Brent Reitz.

Hutchinson, Derek. *Derek C. Hutchinson's Guide to Expedition Kayaking on Sea & Open Water* Third Edition. Old Saybrook CT: Globe Pequot, 1999.

Jacobson, Cliff. *The Basic Essentials of Knots for the Outdoors*. Old Saybrook CT: Globe Pequot, 1999.

Johnson, Shelley. *The Complete Sea Kayaker's Handbook*. Camden ME: Ragged Mountain Press, 2002.

Knapp, Andy. *The Optimum Kayak: How to Choose, Maintain, Repair, and Customize the Right Boat for You*. Camden, ME: Ragged Mountain Press, 2000.

Kulczycki, Chris. *The Kayak Shop: Three Elegant Wooden Kayaks Anyone Can Build*. Camden ME: Ragged Mountain Press, 1993.

Matthews, Alex. *Sea Kayaking: Rough Waters*. Beachburg ON: The Heliconia Press, 2006.

Moores, Ted and Greg Rossel. *Kayaks You Can Build: An Illustrated Guide to Plywood Construction*. Toronto: Firefly Books, 2004.

Moyer, Lee. *Sea Kayak Navigation Simplified*. Mukilteo, WA: Alpen Books, 2001.

ON Nature magazine.

Paddler magazine.

Paddlinginstructor.com [On-line] David Johnston

Sea Kayaker magazine

Seidman, David. *The Essential Sea Kayaker: A Complete Guide for the Open-Water Paddler*. Second Edition. Camden ME: Ragged Mountain Press, 2001.

Superior Outdoors magazine

Sea Kayaking: The Ultimate Guide [Video]. Produced by Ken Whiting and Alex Matthews.

University of Sea Kayaking (USK) [Video Series]. Produced by Wayne Horodowich.

Wave Length Paddling magazine

ORGANIZATIONS

American Canoe Association (www.americancanoe.org)
British Canoe Union North America (www.bcuna.com)
British Canoe Union (www.bcu.org.uk)
Canadian Canoe Museum (www.canadiancanoemuseum.net)
Canadian Coast Guard (www.ccg-gcc.gc.ca)
Canadian Hydrographic Service (www.charts.gc.ca/pub/)
CPAWS Canadian Parks and Wilderness Society (www.cpaws.org)
Earthroots (www.earthroots.org)
Environment Canada Weatheroffice (www.weatheroffice.gc.ca)
Hiawatha Water Trail (www.hiawathawatertrail.org)
The Lake Superior Conservancy and Watershed Council (www.lscwc.org)
Leave No Trace (www.lnt.org)
National Weather Service (www.weather.gov)
The Nature Conservancy (www.nature.org)
The Nature Conservancy of Canada (www.natureconservancy.ca)
Ontario Tourism and Ontario Parks (www.ontariotravel.net/outdoor)
Paddle Canada (www.paddlingcanada.com)
WWWTide and Current Predictor (http://tbone.biol.sc.edu/tide/sitesel.html)
Western Wilderness Committee (www.wildernesscommittee.org)
World of Maps (www.worldofmaps.com)
World Wildlife Fund (www.wwf.ca).

TO ALL OF THE FOLLOWING INDIVIDUALS AND COMPANIES, we have appreciated your faith in our kayaking book project, and also thank you for your various individual efforts to incorporate green ethics into the outdoor industry.

Buff Grubb, Kelley Woolsey and the team at Confluence Watersports, who have steadfastly supported the production of this book with Wilderness Systems kayaks and associated equipment. Lindsay Merchant at North Water Safety Equipment, who makes outstanding watersports safety equipment including towing systems and deck bags. Joe Matuska at Aquabound Paddles, for providing us with a variety of high-quality carbon fiber paddles including child-sized ones to use on our journeys. Steve McNamara and the friendly staff of Kokotat Watersports, for making available the best Gortex drysuits, wetsuits and paddlesports clothing for comfort on and off the water. Dana Nelson and Benoît Deshayes at In-Sport Fashion, who have supported us with the very best Mountain Hardwear tents, sleeping bags and outwear on our wilderness journeys through all four seasons. Brian Dorfman at Grey Owl Paddles, whose wood paddles we have enjoyed for 25 years. Dan Cooke at Cooke Custom Sewing, for making excellent camp shelters. Kent Hering at Littlbug Enterprises, for his low-impact wood-burning campstoves. Dave (Smitty) Smith at Subspace Communications, for satellite phone support. Frank Bryant of Chota Outdoor Gear, for designing those paddling Mukluks that actually keep our feet warm and dry in the coldest, dampest environments. Uwe Mummenhoff, Michael Mayzel and the helpful staff at DayMen Photo, for their on-going support of our photographic expeditions by supplying us with LowePro camera bags, Pelican cases, and digital products from SanDisk and Digipower. Bud Shirley and Helyn Webb of BlueRiver Trading, friends who have been long-time journey supporters with SmartWool, Clif Bar, AlpineAire, Steripen and Sherpani. André Gagnon at C.I.L. Orion, for providing us with a comprehensive array of signaling equipment for Chapter 9. Mid-Canada Fiberglass, for supplying the useful Paddleboy portaging cart to share with our readers in Chapter 5. Alex Tilley, for the greatest hats and so much more. Paul Gorodko of Canada Portable Kayaks, for providing the terrific Pacific Action sail rig, and Bart Boelryk, for the use of the KayRak, both shown in Chapter 13. Gord Espeseth and Janna Espeseth at Trak Kayak, who make the fastest put-together kayaks we have ever paddled. Such kayaks play an important role in making paddling accessible to those who (a) have only enough storage room for a golf bag, (b) use public transportation and rental cars or (c) don't have roof racks.

To friends and family for all the ways you have contributed to making this book a reality, our heartfelt thanks. Peter Pestolozzi of Odyssey Kayaks, who so bravely said he would help us build Greenland kayaks. Thank you, Jeanne Bourquin and Peter, for making this project a reality. Greg and Jeanne Wright, Mark Hansen and the staff of North House Folk School, who so graciously accommodated our family in order to build the kayaks. Herb Wills and Sonja Helland, for their generous hospitality while we built the kayaks. Jeff Elgie and Lucidia Studios, for supporting our on-going conservation efforts on Lake Superior. Steve Bruno, who said that paddling on Lake Superior with us took the wrinkles out of his soul. Sam Crowley, Tim Dyer, Wendy Grater, Gail Green, Grant Herman, Claudia Kerckhoff-VanWijk, Mike Petzold, Dave Tamblyn, Dave Wells, Rick Wise, for their wonderful influence in the kayaking world as guides and instructors. My wonderful parents, John and Jennifer Wood, who introduced me to paddling at a young age, and who are now the best grandparents Sila could ever ask for! Friends Irene Alexander and Ruth O'Gawa, who are always there with an encouraging word or a good idea. My sister, Vivian, and her husband, Tim Alexander, and Sila's cousins, Mirabai and Fae, who provided a great north shore base camp in the Rossport Islands for photographing many of the how-to images. Andrew Haill, Dave MacGillivray and Tarmo Poldmaa, who helped us photograph the tandem maneuvers and rescue recoveries in Chapters 8 and 10. And finally, we could never have assembled all this material into a book without the amazing talents and good humor of our editor, Kathy Fraser, and our designer, Chris McCorkindale.

INDEX